Cognitive Behavioral Therapy

Gain Happiness Using CBT to Remove Anxiety, PTSD, Depression, and Other Negative Thoughts through Positive Thinking (Goal Setting, Killing Bad Habits And Procrastination)

Table Of Contents

Chapter 5: Working on Specifically Anxiety, Negativity, and Stress 56

Treating Anxiety Disorders 56

Chapter 6: Working on Specifically Anger and Depression 68

When is Anger a Problem? 68

What is Unhelpful Angry Behaviour? 69

Preparation 70

Steps to Take in Managing Anger 71

Introduction

You may have heard about it or not, but Cognitive Behavioral Therapy (CBT) is there and has been in use for quite a long time. You may also not know what it means, but you can land on the meaning of the three words to get familiar with this form of therapy.

If you have been to a therapy session before, then whoever was handling you knows about it and at one point maybe suggested it if they did not use it. Also, if you have heard someone talking about how a specific self-help book or therapist helped them recognize their negative thoughts and fears before knowing how to alter them, then you have already heard about the power of using CBT in peoples' lives.

One of the tools found in the psychology store is CBT. The main focus is how mental health and how we behave and feel are interconnected, and how changing one affects the rest. When put into practice, as we will see, there are all manner of outcomes from a broad range of solved problems based on one principle cycle.

Why Recommend CBT?

While it is not the sole solution to mental health and behavioural problems, it is a significant tool that is useful in helping people identify their problems and developing strategies that will help them challenge what they feel and find ways to counter those issues. It takes time to practice but the theory behind it that it is shorter than other forms of therapy seeking to solve the same.

CBT is a tool to help you address the emotional aspects of your life. Here is how:

- It can help you manage mental illness symptoms

- It aids in treating mental illnesses that did not improve while under medication

- Preventing deterioration of mental illness

- Learning how to cope with stressful situations

- How to manage our emotions

- Dealing with loss or grief

- Resolve conflicts in our lives and find better ways of passing information

- Coping with serious physical illnesses

- Going beyond your trauma after a past violence or abuse case

Here are some mental disorders that CBT can address:

- Depression

- Negativity

- Sleeping difficulty

- Bipolar issues

- Sexual disorders

- Anxiety

- Panic attacks

- Eating disorders

- Phobia

- Substance use

- OCD (Obsessive-Compulsive Disorder)

- Schizophrenia

- Overcoming your fears

- Intrusive thoughts

- Guilt

- Bad habits

As you read on, you will also notice that CBT works effectively when combined with other forms of therapy or treatment techniques. In severe cases, that may call for a professional and medication, so if it reaches such a point, seek the appropriate help as you read on.

The Cost of CBT

It depends on how you view it and the intensity of the situation you are trying to solve. For people who can read and understand before contemplating what is going on in their lives, the cost comes down to the price of a self-help book that will guide you through.

On the other hand, when it is severe, and you need the help of a professional, your insurance coverage can handle that if it includes psychotherapy and behavioural treatments. If you are paying straight out of your pocket, then there is a broad range of clinics which either provides the service for free or at a cost, up to $200 per session if you are attending private meetings.

That is why this self-help is available – to help you cope with your difficulties at a lesser cost than the therapist will charge you.

CBT Techniques to Use Outside Therapy Sessions

You are familiar with how to keep a diary or journal, right? Have you ever monitored how you sleep or go out for some fries? Have you ever tracked your thoughts to notice the thinking pattern?

If you have already done that over the course of your life, then you have used some CBT techniques without your knowledge. Here, you will find all the useful methods that CBT utilizes when tailoring behavioural therapy. They will help you allocate time for yourself, capture the problems, challenge them, and then find the feasible solutions before setting the goals.

Why is this Book for You?

We often experience difficulties in our lives, and some of them are listed in the top part of this introduction. This self-help book aims to pair you with some tools that will help you identify your problems and have some skills to manage and manoeuvre them. The tools we have used are based on Cognitive Behavioral Therapy, whose definition and the in-depth cover is in the next chapter.

While reading, you will notice that the book has some intermediate exercises to help you understand the theory between the lines. These exercises will not only help you understand the art of solving mental and behavioural issues but also aid you in doing the homework before the concluding chapter. So, the homework at the end of it all is based on what we have already learned.

If you remember how we went about solving mathematical problems, then the same analogy applies here. The assignments and tables to fill in between the chapters are our practice exercises while the homework is a lengthy exam to help you capture what you have learnt.

Some exercises may not be relevant to you depending on what you are looking to address. The advice here is to focus on what will help you based on what you want to solve. Once you capture the tools that you need to use more, work on them to realize a happier you again.

Welcome!

Do you have any of the problems listed at the top of the introduction? Can you read, understand, and ponder your issues without the help of a therapist? Have you tried other forms of therapy and medication, but they did not work on solving your problem? Are you looking for a way to live happy again without worrying too much?

Then this self-help book is for you. Go ahead to learn the art of CBT, and how you can use it to solve mental and behavioral problems before they become a bother to everyone.

Chapter 2: Cognitive Behavioral Therapy

What is CBT?

Mental health is paramount in the way we conduct ourselves. That is why CBT (Cognitive Behavioral Therapy) takes a step to change how we think, the beliefs that hold us back knowingly or unknowingly, our attitude towards various issues affecting our lives, and how we behave when facing challenging situations, not forgetting the strive to achieve our set objectives.

Adjusting your negative thoughts using this form of therapy does not need to take your whole lifetime. Those who receive it from their therapists know that it takes utmost, ten months with 50-60 minutes per session once a week. While we can view it as a hands-on approach that requires you and the professional to be available, sometimes it's overwhelming to see you juggle your mind in front of someone who is continuously looking at their watch.

> The idea here is that our mode of thinking, behaving and feeling is what makes us experience what we go through

That is why we give you a solution that you can use while at home.

This does not mean that you should ignore professional help when presented. If you can read and are able to identify what is troubling your mind, therapists may not be necessary after going to that quiet spot a few times a week just like in therapy.

A Little History About Cognitive Behavioral Therapy

Aaron Beck is the name behind this form of therapy. In the 60's, this man was busy working on psychoanalysis on his patients. During the analysis, he noted something strange and unusual. They seemed to have an *inner dialogue* going on in their minds, as if they had someone else talking to them in there or were merely talking to themselves internally. When Beck enquired about their thinking status, the patients only produced a portion of the total information.

To give an example, the patient in his office was probably thinking, "The therapist is super quiet today. Am I boring him, or does he have a lot on his mind to ponder?" The first sentence of thought triggered the second one, and this is how such an internal dialogue starts. After some time, the client would think, "Maybe my issues are not that important to this high-end figure." At this point, he or she will not adequately communicate their real feelings.

That is when Beck came to know that something connected one's feelings and thoughts. He went ahead to come up with the phrase **automatic thoughts** to signify the ideas overwhelmed by emotions that come abruptly to mind without the knowledge of the victim. While it may not be possible for the client to know what is happening in their brain, there is a way to identify them and report when they occur.

By identifying such thinking modes, the client would then be able to understand what is happening to them and eventually overcome the hurdles in life.

That is when Cognitive Behavioral Therapy was born. The primary purpose was to place the importance of thinking at the forefront of solving our problems. The terms cognitive and behavior are joined together since apart from the mind, behavioral techniques also need to be addressed. A balance between the two varies depending on other forms of therapy using CBT as the main basis, but they are all defined under this form of treatment.

Today, it has undergone various professional trials all over the world in a bid to solve mind and behavior related problems.

CBT in Depth

Cognitive Behavioral Therapy represents a goal-oriented psychological therapy treatment whose hands-on approach drives towards problem-solving. The objective here is to change our thinking patterns or the behavioral aspects that bring about the difficulties which will eventually replace the focus of our feelings. If you looked at the introduction, there are many problems that this form of therapy can address, from sleeping troubles to anxiety, depression, and drug abuse.

Using CBT means finding a way to change the patient's attitude and how they respond to situations by shedding light on the beliefs, images, and thoughts held in the cognitive process. In that way, the victim can focus and be able to deal with emotional situations.

Think of it as a combination of behavioral therapy and psychotherapy. The latter focusses on the meaning we use on what we come across in our lives and how the thinking pattern started when we were little. Behavioral therapy, on the other hand, digs into the relationship available between our thoughts and problems and how we behave.

The following diagram will show you how the things mentioned above are interconnected. We will then focus on it by applying various life situations that will pick the same pattern as depicted below.

SCENARIO

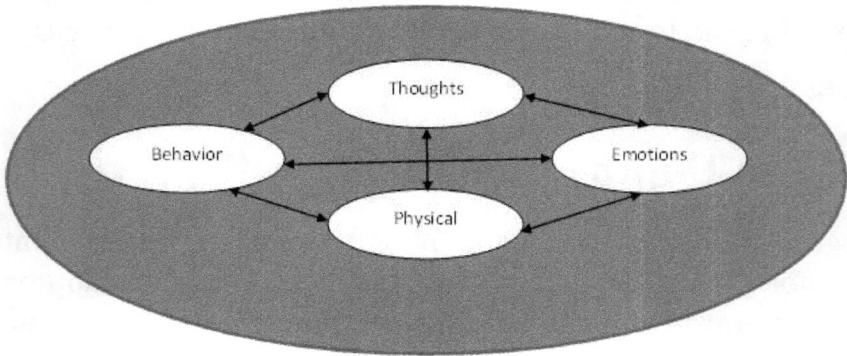

CBT Principles

Since it includes learning essential skills that will help us manage what makes us feel down, you will possess new methods of behaving and thinking as you look forward to controlling your situation in the future. Here are a few things you need to understand when using CBT.

This Form of Therapy Focuses on the Present

We must dig into the past to get the cause of what is happening to us. On the other hand, CBT treatment will focus on the symptoms that are currently driving you in the wrong direction and not where it all began. So, for example, if you are dealing with anxiety, knowing where it all started is not enough to help you cope.

> **Take it this way:** If you are terrified every time you see someone stronger than you, the main reason is that you fear the stiff competition and back in your mind. Chances are that they will outshine you in whatever you are contesting together. If you check the background, the cause might be being bullied when you were young. That will definitely make you fear the mighty ones.
>
> **What's the problem:** Even after knowing the sole reason behind your fear, it does not exclude the idea of frightening every time you see more muscles or brains around you.

Homework is Essential

Whether it comes from a therapist or this self-help book,

homework is vital. Doing the assignments given means that you will have something to do every week and you need to practice what you learn by applying the skills daily. Since it is homework, you need to keep using what you have gained until it sticks in your mind.

Necessitating the need for practice is not enough, so you need something more than motivation. Unless you learn to practice the things you have learnt, what is most likely to happen is that you'll forget after some time. When you are later facing your problem, it will be hard to remember how to utilize the skills.

Learning the new methods can be compared to gaining a new habit, healthy to be precise.

If you need to start jogging in the morning, it might appear hard in the first few days, but after a few trials, it will become part of your routine. CBT applies the same notion. If you make it a habit to practice what will make you change the way you think and act, you'll soon get used to it so, the more you are into it, the easier it gets.

What You Learn In CBT

First, you will learn how to change the way you think and how you behave after thinking. Remember it is a behavioral therapy that is based on cognition. The reason why it is vital is that at any given instance, thoughts, feelings, and behavior are always interconnected. Each of the aspects fuels the rest and the cycle continues until you deal with one or all of them.

Back to our example of fearing the stronger ones – imagine a situation where you meet the person who always needs something from you before entering your neighborhood. The expectation here is too much fear as you ponder what to do. Since he will be on your neck until you meet his demands, you must find another route even though it's a long one, or give him what he wants.

Referring to the interconnection diagram, here is how it would look:

MEETING THE BULLY

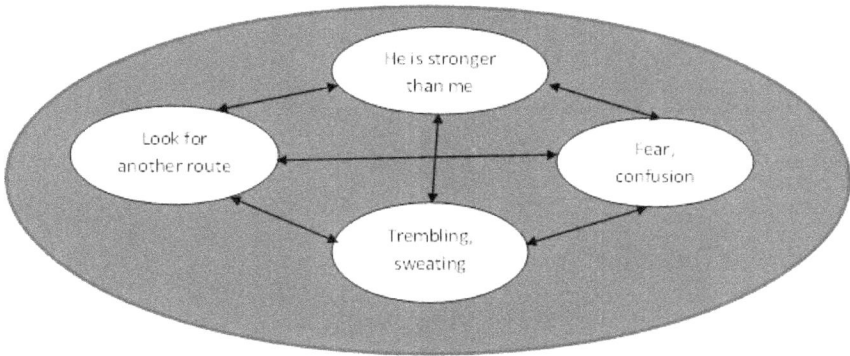

However, if one thinks of a way to settle the matter with the big friend, he might buy an idea that works for him, or use something that will make sure he never gets in your way. By saying something, please think about the legal means, instead of doing something stupid. Now, let's get back to our pattern. It will look differently, like this:

MEETING THE BULLY

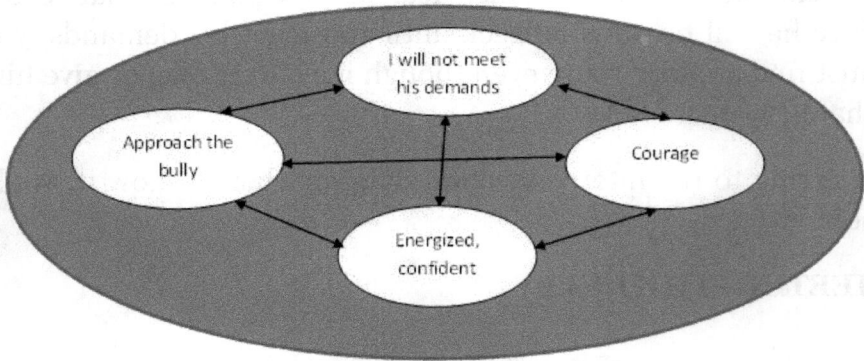

With that in mind, one can decide to use the following options to manage the bully:

Option 1: Change the Mode of Behavior

First, going around the situation to use a method that makes the friend weak, there will be something to tell him and a way to calm everything down on the victim's side. After that, it will be evident in the mind that we are all humans and sometimes we act rationally or irrationally depending on the circumstance. That way, one gets exposed to the person before going ahead to know them by having a conversation that will calm the fear later.

Even though movies are just pictured stories, we can learn this from the stars in the end after they cope with the task at hand.

Option 2: Change the Mode of Thinking

It is also possible to challenge the thoughts by thinking about the reason behind the fear for the bully. One will remember later that it is because you don't want to find yourself in a situation where you'll have to meet his demands. That way, you will be able to know that you don't have to give them what they need if it's not your gate pass.

The reason why we let such fear drive us is that we think negatively on how we have to submit if we meet the person. After that, it's possible to feel threatened and get blinded from seeing the whole picture. Since you are afraid, it is possible to always think about the harm that might get in the way instead of what will make them turn around and leave you alone. If one's thoughts are well balanced, things and situations are seen under a clear vision, which provides the mind with the necessary tools to address the fear.

Are There Pros And Cons In CBT?

While it is as effective as the medication used when treating valid mental disorders, one man's meat is another man's poison, so it may not suit every psychologically-driven behavior.

The advantages include:

- Time taken can be relatively shorter than other forms of therapy.

- It can be the only solution where medication is not working.

- There are many ways of presenting it, which include using a therapist, getting self-help books, or using apps.

- The skills taught are practical when applied in everyday life even after therapy.

The disadvantages include:

- There is a need for more cooperation and commitment since it is a long process.

- Much time consumption especially if it involves a therapist and extra work to be done.

- There is a confrontation of emotions and thoughts here so, during the beginning, one is bound to experience some uncomfortable form of anxiety.

- Complex mental issues may need further assistance and treatment. At such a point, CBT may not be of good use.

This is What You Need to Remember

- CBT is research-based, so there is proof that it works.

- CBT teaches us new thinking and behaving ways. This is a self-help book that can help you with that.

- What we think, feel, and behave are all in a cycle, so they are interconnected. Changing one means affecting the rest.

Chapter 3: Identify and Evaluate

A human being is structured in a way that he or she is not to be confined by his or her influences, whether biological or environmental. Preferably, a human is structured to be actively involved in the designing and actualization of his or her desired reality or destiny, as many would like to call it. This, believe it or not, starts in the brain or just the thoughts of an individual.

To back this statement is a quote from Buddha that states, "We are what we think". This statement means that our actions are dependent on our thoughts – the core of **cognitive behavioral therapy.** For one to understand what emotions he or she has to a particular event, it is essential first to discover what he or she thinks about that event or radically the meanings he or she attaches to what is happening. It may not seem that important, but people are usually different.

For example, a person who has lost their job may find it hard to go on with life because of an increased burden on his or her shoulders, and thus may end up getting depressed. On the other hand, another person in the same situation may find this relieving. This is because maybe he or she did not find the working environment conducive. This person may even adopt a celebratory mood. Can you see the difference in response to the same situation?

The one thing that one notices from the above example is that the effect of an event can simply be changed by the way we think about it. That is why you'll need guidance through CT (cognitive therapy). Cognitive therapy gives one a wide variety of ways to think about what is affecting them. Even in the worst of cases, one will have several viewpoints on how one can view the situation. It is like when a person dies and the bereaved, instead of mourning the deceased death, start praising him or even celebrate a life well lived.

How many of us do that?

Information processing becomes distorted when we experience emotional distress

To start with, what is the meaning of emotional distress? It is an unpleasant feeling that usually affects our thinking. Anxiety, stress, and depression are all types of emotional distresses. These distress forms are normal to human beings.

However, they can become problematic when one cannot manage his or her feelings, and this can lead to cognitive lapses. That is where cognitive therapy comes in handy. CT is usually based on an information-processing model that merely depicts the fact that when one is going through some emotional distress, he or she tends to overthink events or, in short, one's judgment becomes distorted.

A good example is when one is about to go to a job interview, he or she tends to accumulate a lot of stress and anxiety on whether they will get the job. This kind of emotional distress can cause one not to be attentive to the interviewers, or may lead one to not answer questions correctly.

Some may ask how emotional distresses affect our thoughts and decisions. This is a relatively simple question to answer. The psychological state of a person can change his or her brain in many ways. The first way is by altering the hormones and neurotransmitters that we rely on to think. These can be modified negatively, making one not think clearly. The second way is through sleep, fatigue, and maybe even headaches.

However, this is usually indirect on the latter.

Dangerous as it may seem, one can be taught how to manage his or her distresses. The primary way to do this is by undergoing cognitive therapy. CT teaches clients first to identify and correct errors associated with these types of judgments. Other recommendable ways to manage these feelings include spending more time with loved ones, indulging in exercises, or having a proper diet every day.

The Importance Of Negative Thoughts

Just as mentioned in the beginning, cognitive behavioral therapy is based on a theory that 'it is not events that determine our feelings but rather the meaning we attach to these events.' This means that if one's thoughts are too negative, they can hinder one from making clear and reliable decisions.

A good example is a student who has not got good grades in a test. This goes without saying that it will make the student get depressed and stressed. However, the decision that the student will make will be determined by how he or she thinks of such an event. Positive thoughts will prepare the student to see that failure as a stepping stone to a higher grade, and thus he or she will work even harder to achieve more.

On the other hand, **negative thoughts** will lead a student to think entirely different about himself or herself or even maybe the world. The student may start thinking that he or she is not capable of anything in life, and this kind of thought often causes one to go to the extreme of committing suicide.

However, strange as it might sound, negative thoughts usually do have some importance. At a closer look, pessimists typically do not face the reality of life as it is. Instead, they try to run away from the fact of life.

Let's take the example above. The student may have decided to have "thought positively" and ask himself or herself "what is the worst that could ever happen?" and later act as if that is the most inspiring advice he or she has ever got. However, this would not be of help because such positive thoughts tend to show us that we have already achieved and thus make us reluctant. The opinion, therefore, does not make us reach or achieve our full potential in life.

Where Do These Negative Thoughts Come From?

It is believed that negative thoughts usually come from beliefs that one was taught during childhood. We then grow up with these beliefs deeply inscribed in us, and they become relatively fixed and automatic. How is this possible?

Let's take for example a child who has been brought up with the virtue that for him or her to be successful in life, he or she must pass in their tests in school. This is a phrase that is quite common for everyone. The expression, however, leads to increased stress in a child because once the child maybe fails, then he or she will start having the negative thoughts of "maybe I am not good enough" or "am I even going to succeed in life after all?" These are some of the negative thoughts that we are talking about. These thoughts often occur naturally and automatically due to the beliefs.

In such cases, a change of beliefs is usually the best cause of action to take to remedy such thoughts. This is where cognitive therapy usually comes in. Cognitive behavioral therapy helps one "think outside the box" in such instances. In the case of the child above, he or she will be able to step out and explore other causes of action to take in case of a test failure.

What is essential to understand in this section is that adverse events are always bound to happen, but the question to ask is how are you going to approach the confrontation?

How Does One Go About Identifying Cognitive Problems?

To start with, cognitive problems, just as you may have noticed, are issues that an individual may encounter with their memory or thinking. There are two ways an individual can deal with such impairments.

Step 1: Recognizing the thoughts made, physical symptoms, or even a change in one's behavior.

Cognitive therapy usually calls for a step by step breakdown of actions to take with the motive of dealing with a cognitive problem. This is because one can take some time while dealing with a problem. Therefore, the breakdown of a plan into small manageable goals is usually indispensable.

A good example to back up this statement is in the case of a test failure by a student. It might prove hard for the student to move directly from the low grade to the higher one. However, it is much easier and more realistic for the student to move from one rank to another until he or she reaches the desired level.

In this step, therefore, one has to evaluate their thoughts, physical symptoms, and even a change in their behavior. Eventually, this will be able to help one ascertain whether or not they are under some emotional distress or not.

To understand this better, we are going to deal with one at a time.

THOUGHTS

These are the things that one thinks about during an event. When one is depressed or anxious, amongst other issues, various thoughts usually cross one's mind. These thoughts typically depend on the situation. The thoughts we are concerned with here are majorly the negative thoughts. They may include:

- I am a failure.

- This is not meant for me.

- I will not succeed.

- I am weak.

When you realize you are having such thoughts, you are under some distress of some kind that is clouding your judgment. How does one get to the bottom of it?

An example of this is by maybe considering:

- What happened?

- What did you think about the situation?

- Was it correct or not?

Try to answer what is causing what you are thinking. Finally, evaluate the answer and compare it to the judgment you would have made while in a sober state or rather the decision you would have come to if the current problem did not tamper the mind.

PHYSICAL SYMPTOMS

The next thing one must check for is the physical symptoms. The physical symptoms we are talking about include:

- Restlessness

- Lack of sleep

- Increased heartbeat

- That feeling of butterflies in the stomach

A majority of people have encountered a number of these physical symptoms, and the leading cause is emotional distress. Therefore, when one notices such problems, be sure that you are under some difficulty, maybe stress or even depression.

A good example is like in the cases of anxiety and stress, where the adrenaline in one's body can cause one to feel hot, sweaty, an increased rate in heartbeat, difficulty in breathing, shaky, increased urge to go to the toilet, and even butterflies in the stomach which could lead to stomach discomfort. On the other hand, in the cases of depression, one feels tired, exhausted, lack of sleep, or even lacks interest in sex.

BEHAVIORAL CHANGE

The last thing that will help one ascertain whether they are under some emotional distress is a change in behavior. Stress and depression are usually associated with some responses which include:

- Distancing oneself from friends and family

- Lack of self-motivation

- A tendency to eat less

An excellent example of this is in the case of depression; one may decide to stay in bed and pull the covers over their head, choose not to go out, not to answer the phone, watch television, or even decline a friend's invite without a solid reason. On the other hand, in the case of anger, one can shout at someone, throw or aimlessly vandalize things around him, beat up someone or something.

Even though we have discussed each factor separately, they are all usually intertwined at some point. Look at it this way, the thought that one is a failure can lead to increased stress which may cause the person to become restless and thus lead to a lack of sleep. The notion that one is a failure may even lead to one thinking that they are not meant to socialize with certain people, and therefore one distances himself or herself with the outside world.

Thus, there is a cycle of negative thoughts, changes in behaviour, and physical symptoms that will keep you emotionally distressed. We will see as we go on.

In the space below, fill in your thoughts, behaviour, and physical symptoms from a situation you are going through.

Thoughts	Behaviour	Physical Symptoms

Now, after writing them down, try to look for the link and write it down in the space below.

Link between your thoughts, behaviour, and physical symptoms

Step 2: Define Your Problem and Set Goals

This step usually follows after one has determined whether he or she has a cognitive problem, as in step one. This step, therefore, helps one define the problem and, most importantly, accept the challenge. While describing the problem, one has to be sober and of clear mind to determine the problem precisely. Instead of just saying that the problem is the stress, one should go more in-depth and establish the cause of your stress. There are several parameters that one should consider while identifying the problem, like:

- What causes the problem?

- Why does the problem affect me?

- When does the problem affect me most?

- Where does the problem occur?

Once you ask yourself these questions, then you will have achieved the second step in dealing with cognitive problems.

In the space provided below, fill in the problems that you have been facing. It could be one or many. In the boxes below each problem, rate the problem in the first box before addressing it, with a scale of 1-10 with satisfaction going up the ladder. Rate it again in the second box after pursuing it, then the last one after one last pursuit to how the progress is moving along.

Identification and evaluation, however, does not end here. One must accept the fact that he or she is facing a particular problem and thus face it head on to solve it.

The best way, therefore, is by setting goals. A goal, here, is what the patient wants to achieve by the end of the therapy. Remember that as you read this, you are the therapist helping yourself to get better. A goal helps in remaining loyal to the course and going ahead to check on the progress for some feedback.

The one trick with setting goals is that one must be as transparent as possible. Instead of saying that by the end of the therapy you want to feel less depressed, be more precise and note down what you would want to do once you are less depressed. Some examples are:

- I would want to go for a road trip somewhere

- I would like to have a cup of coffee quietly

- I would like to visit a specific place

These goals can be very enticing while writing them down, but it is good to have just a few goals so as not to make it cumbersome while achieving them.

Now, write down your goals in the space below and rate them after every month in the boxes below depending on how you are progressing to achieve them. Use the scale of 1-10.

Goal 1

Goal 2

After all of the above has been done, then you will have successfully moved a significant step towards healing oneself. Acting as your therapist is not comfortable, but following the steps carefully makes you conquer your liabilities. Just like that.

> This is the primary objective of this book. To help you treat yourself at the comfort of your home while the therapist watches subtly.

Before concluding this chapter, cognitive impairment is majorly a disease that affects the elderly due to a condition called dementia. However, this does not rule out the fact that it may affect anyone irrespective of their age. Therefore, older people should be treated with much more care. This condition can, however, be avoided by maybe avoiding major head injuries and even regularly exercising one's brain. It can be done by indulging in brain games like chess or solving puzzles.

Chapter 4: Killing Negative Thoughts

or Beliefs

Changing our old habits needs us to examine more of what we think. To manage what we need to change, we need to check the aspect of negative thinking and how it affects our daily decision-making.

Only then will the victimized find glory by shedding off the negative thoughts and creating room for new positive ones. At that point, we can now begin to condition the brain to adapt to the new positive environment.

It is essential to address the issue of negative automatic thoughts (NATs). Before that, here is an overview of thoughts and other things that go on in our minds.

Our Thoughts Overview

What are They?

They are what go through our minds. They include what we believe in, the standards we want to live by, our ethics and morals, what we believe to be, and what the world feeds us.

Self-Talk

We are not always aware of this, but we always store and interpret what goes on in our lives. People constantly think about what surrounds or affects them as if there is someone else inside who is communicating to them. Those who are good in psychology will say that the inner voice we hear is 'self-talk.' It happens in all of us, but within our minds so, it deserves the name. Self-talk involves the conscious thoughts and unconscious ones too.

Thoughts Affect our Feelings

What we hold in our minds, from attitude to beliefs, have a significant effect on how we interpret what happens in our lives. In short, our feelings are depicted by our thoughts. If one learns how to stay positive based on the associated motivations that nature provides, there will be much pleasure to enjoy afterwards. Vice versa will happen too if we engage in negative thoughts.

It is almost Impossible to Control our Thoughts

Whether you want to shut out the bad thought or not, just like good ones, it will come and go. Thoughts are merely what you are interpreting from the outside world, and they will be moving in and out as long as you are awake and alive.

What we Think is not Necessarily the Reality

We learn from the environment and our interpretation of what we see. With that, there is a reason why we should not trust what we think 100%. There are individual biases to our experiences in life that will also influence our thinking and interpretation. We eventually attach what we have resulted to meanings of the happening, future or past events, but that does not mean that what we know is correct.

Error in Thinking

Sometimes, we think about the wrong thing – it could be long-term or something that pops up from time to time. Such thoughts will prevent you from making the right scrutiny in what you go through; hence, the wrong decision. That is when you see yourself appearing on the wrong road to decision making, thinking irrationally and judging fast, or even worse, assuming the worst-case scenarios. Such errors in thinking are also known as cognitive distortions since they come with twisted perspectives on how to deal with things.

Thoughts are Automatic

This is where the **Negative Automatic Thoughts** come in – as part of automatic views. They always pop into our heads without our knowledge, and they have no warning either. They are distorted forms of thinking, and they provide unhelpful ways of thinking and interpreting events. That is why they are **harmful.** Most of us who suffer from such will not know when they come and may not even be aware that they are actually negative. If they are frequent, they become familiar to the person to the point of not questioning them on whether they are helpful or appropriate in the first place.

Here is an example of NATs:

- "Everybody hates me."

- "Nothing is ever right no matter what I do."

- "I will lose the opportunity if I'm late."

- "I don't think I'm intelligent."

Is There a Difference Between Thoughts and Emotions?

Yes, there is a difference. Thoughts come in structures, so you can view that as they come in a sentence or a statement. You think about a combination of factors back in the mind before the final thought comes out, and that is why it involves some things.

Emotions are different in that we describe them using one word, angry or depressed. So, people who are anxious are experiencing that as a feeling and not as a thought. Some statements from back in the mind are leading to anxiousness.

Now, we need to focus on how we can change the negative thinking to a positive one and sticking there. We need to let go of the negativity in our brains so that there is room for better and honest thoughts.

Here, we are going to deploy three strategies in dealing with our thoughts. You can call them the thought challenging techniques.

- Strategy one: Catching the negative thoughts or beliefs

- Strategy two: Finding the relevant evidence

- Strategy three: Finding an alternative view based on the evidence

Now, let us see how these strategies work.

Strategy One: Catching the Negative Thoughts or Beliefs

We are not used to capturing the negative thoughts, especially if they just pop in and go. That is why it can be hard to do so. With that, we need to find time to practice this technique so that we can record them whenever they appear. In case you have more than one thought that is disturbing you, try to see which thought causes the 'bad thought.' When you have it, see how firmly you believe in it using a scale of 0-100%.

So that you can capture your thoughts, here are some questions that you need to ask yourself. You can go ahead and formulate such questions for your thoughts.

What are your surroundings?

- What was the activity before thinking?

- Who was around at the time?

- What were you thinking at that time?

- What is the worst thing you have ever thought about?

- What picture does it draw about you in case it's true?

Now, as you try to capture the NATs, here is something that you need to remember:

- They appear as short instances, and they are also particular

- They come in rapidly after a situation or event

- They mostly come in words or images

- You don't think that way from a careful perspective

- There is no particular order in which they occur

- At the time of thinking, they can appear as reasonable

Trapping Your Thoughts

As you try to capture NATs, it is possible to identify the theme of negative thinking. If you haven't heard of cognitive distortions and what they are, here is a description for you:

Thinking All or Nothing

This is where everything is this or that. Nothing in the middle. Something is either done to the level best, or it is a total mess. It may also apply to people where you either love someone entirely or hate them.

Over-Generalizing Issues

If you see something going south and you don't like it at all, you attach the same results to all other similar events. It also happens to people, where if someone is vindictive, you interpret that all people who look like him appear that way.

Filtering Your Thoughts

This happens when you take a particular situation and dwell on the negative side of things for a long time. That makes you equalize everything that occurs as negative.

Getting Rid of the Positive

Here, you shun out every real detail that is vital to what you are experiencing since you see them as not helpful for one reason or the other. That way, you stick to a negative form of thinking that contradicts your daily experiences.

Jumping into Conclusions

It involves making adverse decisions even with no absolute facts that support what you have concluded. It also includes weird mind reading where you reach a decision such as people are not reacting positively towards you, but you don't go ahead to follow up on what's the matter. At times, it comes to foretelling that events will turn out negative basing your prediction as a fact.

Catastrophizing

After thinking that something is entirely wrong, it is possible to start exaggerating the essence of the situation. That is where you arrive at constraining your achievements or capabilities.

Reasoning through Emotions

Since you have some negative feelings, you associate that with the way things appear. If you think that you can't achieve something, then you go ahead and believe that it is entirely impossible.

Enacting What You Should or Must Do

Moving towards setting objectives of what you think you should be doing. They are often high and unachievable despite the force you use to push yourself. If you don't achieve, where in most cases that is what happens, you find yourself overcoming to guilt. It also happens when you direct the **must and should** phrases to people, and in the end, you feel angry and frustrated.

Attaching Labels and the Wrong Ones too

It is a form of generalization that goes to the extreme ends. Instead of seeing your faults, you give yourself a label that you are the worst. If someone's behavior is not the best and it agitates you, you move on by giving them a tag, 'he is just weird.' When it comes to attaching the wrong tag, you tend to use language that is always loaded with emotions.

Personalization

You see yourself as the cause of some negative action in an event or the cause of the whole negative situation. Most likely, you are not even associated with what happened, despite naming yourself as the main culprit.

Assignment 1

Think about the unhelpful ways you think about or use to think negatively. Do you notice a pattern?

My unhelpful thinking ways

What will you do the next time you notice their presence?

I will try to...

Assignment 2

So that we can successfully capture our negative thoughts and
see how they affect our emotions and behavior, we need a diary

to hold them accountable every time they appear.

On the following page is a personal diary for you to fill in. We will start with an example first.

Situation	Emotions	Catching NATs
What location? *What was the activity?* *Who was present?* *Time of occurrence?*	*What are your feelings?* *Intensity by percentage*	*What popped up in your mind?* *What bad things do you think will happen?* *Intensity by percentage* *Can you associate it with an unhelpful way of thinking?*
I did not finish my work today. I had three days to do it.	Low by 90% Stressed by 100% Confused by 80%	I will not get through this – 70% I'm a terrible worker – 80% I should tell my boss that I cannot make it up to him – 75% I'm a total failure – 95%

You can fill in yours, using the example in the previous page.

Situation	Emotions	Catching NATs
What location? *What was the activity?* *Who was present?* *Time of occurrence?*	*What are your feelings?* *Intensity by percentage*	*What popped up in your mind?* *What bad things do you think will happen?* *What is the overall image on you?* *Intensity by percentage* *Can you associate it with an unhelpful way of thinking?*

Strategy Two: Finding the Relevant Evidence

After capturing the NATs, this stage will help you challenge the negative thoughts. The process of confrontation is based on checking the evidence against and for a particular thought.

Here are some questions that you can ask yourself in your evidence quest:

- What view would someone else share about the same situation?

- If I wasn't this way at all, would I view it the same way?

- What other view can a person use in the same situation?

What Help do We Get from Challenging our Thoughts?

Getting balanced thoughts implies having a better chance at functioning more appropriately. Soon, you will realize that you are enjoying life experiences again. We think our thoughts or opinions. There is no scientific evidence that people utilize to arrive at a certain thought and, since you are thinking, that does not necessarily mean that it is true. The evidence is based on the subject, so there might be some complexity involved when trying to prove.

If we get the factual evidence about something, then there is no room for doubt. Evidence based on facts is object-oriented, so disproving it is impossible. We want to challenge our thoughts, right? Then we need to practice a way of looking for evidence against or for the 'bad thought.' The idea here is to work with the

43

thought that drives you to do what you do or causes emotional distress. This thought should have the highest rating of belief. Now, after getting the thought and relevant evidence, we can comfortably look for a countering thought that works based on the evidence.

Look at the following diary that directs you on how to challenge your thoughts.

Assignment 3

Here is an example of an addict who thinks that they must be on their drug or alcohol to solve stress in life and function 'appropriately' based on their thinking. Do you remember the 3-column diary we had to challenge the bad thoughts? We will use that as a guideline.

Negative thought: I have to drink before facing her in the evening. This is too much.

Evidence for	Evidence Against	Thoughts based on evidence *The helpful thoughts*	Revising what we feel *How do you feel now?* *What's your cause of action?*
I did not meet her	I love her, so I have to be	I'm not a bad person and I have to go and	Alcohol craving? 60%

| expectations.

I have not been home for a while. | there for her.

We can always solve issues if I present myself.

I have to fix it if I'm to be happy again. | resolve the matter.

I don't have to drink to explain myself. That would also cause chaos. | Stressed? 50%

Hot and sweaty? 70% |

Now, it's time to fill in yours.

Negative thought:

Evidence for	Evidence against	Thought based on evidence *The helpful thoughts*	Revising what we feel *How do you feel now?* *What's your cause of action?*

Strategy Three: Finding an Alternative Thought Based on the Evidence

In strategy two, we used CBT to confront our negative thoughts by looking for evidence on both ends. In strategy three, we will be creating a new thought that will act as an alternative to the 'bad thought' and it must appear as a positive working solution when compared to the previous one.

We need to note that the new thought does not mean that it is the opposite of negativity. CBT may be centered on developing positive thinking, but we should view it as helping you to have a balanced way of thinking.

Check the diagram below to verify the meaning of the above statement.

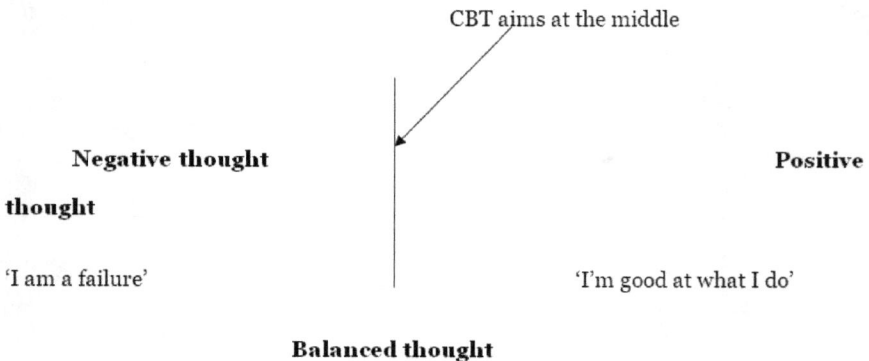

CBT aims at the middle

Negative thought   **Positive thought**

'I am a failure'   'I'm good at what I do'

Balanced thought

"I might not be able to handle the task at hand, but with the right help and commitment, I can conquer the test."

To summarize how it works, once you capture the NATs, look at the other end of the line and think about the other extreme case. So, it's from extreme negative to extreme positive. After getting the two variables, try to come into the middle by having a balanced thought based on the collected evidence.

Case Study

Picture yourself as a judge or magistrate in court. You have a defendant on one side who is accused of being a peddler, selling illegal drugs on the street. To present some evidence in the name of innocence, he says that he was not there, and he does not do that. The prosecutors are holding him accountable and they have CCTV footage showing him doing the trade for an hour or so.

As the judge, what decision will you make and what do you think about the outcome?

Challenging our thoughts is like being the judge in a case. The defendant can be seen as the 'bad thoughts' which represents seeing yourself as a failure. The evidence presented to support failure is because you just know it. On the other hand, does that justify your thinking? Is it strong enough to live by? Once you consider the evidence at hand, construct a verdict for the case using the evidence for an alternative thought.

Assignment 4

Here is a diary for your thoughts. Find some time and complete it if you are ready to capture some negative thoughts in your life. Remember what we discussed above when collecting the evidence for and against the thoughts. It could be one or many. You can draw a table that resembles the same if you have more thoughts to capture.

What is the situation?	Describe your emotions with one word	What are the automatic negative thoughts?	Evidence for	Evidence against	An alternative thought based on the evidence	Rate your emotions with a scale of 0-100%

Are There Strategies to Challenge Negative Thoughts?

So far, we have covered the most important section about knowing what negative thoughts are, and how to counter them while developing positive ones. They can be hard to capture, but once you have done it, you can start to develop new ways of thinking that enable you to balance your thoughts.

Here are some strategies to help you cope as you drive into the world of positive thinking.

Thoughts have One Name: 'Thoughts'

Whether negative or positive, they are just what they are. You can view them as commercials after a news break or the annoying internet pop-ups on every other page you land on.

Do Something that You can be Proud of

Negative thoughts can be helpful in beating yourself up, but they still come, so you are hurting yourself by punishing yourself all the time. Instead, use the time to accomplish something vital that can help you or give you the pride of accomplishment. If it's something you are good at, the better.

Make Use of Your Worries

Too much negative thinking will drive you towards not realizing your goals and being unproductive almost all the time. You are always thinking about the negatives, but you cannot see what you need to do to fix it. In that case, use your brain power to solve your problems and use solutions that you can work with.

Verify the Worst, Best, and What is Most Likely to Happen

When a situation consumes you to the verge of negative thinking, ask yourself about the best outcome, the worst outcome, and what is likely to happen. That way, you will be viewing the situation from all angles, and also be prepared if there is a mixture of the two extremes. Remember the diagram about where CBT aims – at the middle of both extremes.

Have the Right Perspective for Your Peace of Mind

In one situation or event, there are always more ways to explain it. If your view is not working for you, or it presents unfavorable scenarios, give yourself a challenge and look for an explanation that works. As you peruse, you will land on the one that helps you rest or get on with your daily activities.

Provide Proof of Negative Thoughts

Earlier in the strategies we talked about finding the evidence. So, if you are still on a defeating clause or thinking pattern, go ahead to seek proof of what makes it false instead of sitting on it.

Involve Someone Else

If you are facing the negative thoughts alone, then it can be hard to completely get rid of them. When there are people around you, such thoughts will tend to pop up less often.

Talk to Yourself Positively

The truth about talking to people and yourself is that you'll never talk to people the way you engage in self-talk. So, instead of seeking a way to talk to people the way you do to yourself, allow self-positive talk so that you can increase the confidence within you. That way, you will have your own support team in you.

Now, are you still facing some thinking errors? Here are some questions to help you identify the thinking mistakes. They are based on how to trap your thoughts.

Questions That Will Help You Identify Negative Thinking

- Am I jumping to the worst conclusions ever?

- Am I overthinking or not thinking about anything at all?

- Am I swearing after realizing the general conclusions from an event?

- Am I foretelling or waiting to see what will go on?

- Am I overthinking what people think about me?

- Am I too focused on the negative such that it overshadows the positive?

- Am I shunning out the positive comments and making them look like negative ones?

- Am I positioning myself as a failure and useless?

- Am I listening too much from the negative side such that I can't make time for the positive vibes?

- Am I taking another's behaviors too personally or do I blame myself for overlooking?

- Do I use forceful language such as 'must' and 'should' to dictate the rules that I should follow?

How do You Go about Finding Evidence against Negative Thinking?

- Do I have previous experience that shows what I think is not true?

- If someone I knew or loved had such a thought, what would I say to them?

- If they knew what I usually think when I'm alone or troubled, what would they say?

- What are they likely to say to oppose what I think and to show that it's not true?

- When I'm not troubled or thinking about the negative side, how would I tackle the same situation that I'm facing?

- In the past, when I felt this way or was approached by such an event, what made me cope and feel relieved?

- Is this the same situation that I have been facing or is there something different about the current one?

- If there are past experiences that are not similar, but they made me feel weird or prompted me to do something stupid, what lessons did I learn that can help me now?

- Are there other things that make me think otherwise and I'm not aware?

- What will happen three years from now? How will I be viewing such a situation?

- What positive things can I deduce from myself or from the situation? Am I ignoring them?

- After jumping to conclusions, are they viable based on the available evidence?

- Do I blame myself for things that I cannot control?

Some Beliefs will not Cause Problems

Before concluding this chapter, if one goes ahead and believes in the notion of a normal human being, then the following beliefs cannot hurt you. Actually, they make you stronger.

I cannot be Loved by Everyone

Thinking that you are not the world's darling is much better than thinking of how good you are for people to love you. On our side, we don't love everyone, so why expect anything different from them? It is okay to enjoy being loved, but if someone doesn't, it's just okay. Remember that we cannot make people love or hate us and they cannot also do the same to us. It is alright to receive disapproval at some point.

I make Mistakes Once in a While

Making mistakes is part of our lives and it's vital since it provides a learning moment. Always know that, as long as it is not something that will restrain your happiness for the rest of your life, you will make mistakes and life will go on despite your upset. If you are still learning, then also learn to accept and move on. It will help you change your behavior and thinking as long you are able to handle yourself. Accept your mistakes and those of others too.

I cannot Control Everything, so I don't have to Control Something

We can survive what appears different to us – it's only a matter of accepting what is beyond our control. If we learn to accept things the way they come, then we can love the people around us no matter how they appear to be, and yourself too. You don't have any requirement to like something or put it the way you like it, so accept what you can't change and live with it.

I'm Responsible for Myself

I'm the one who declares what I feel and what to do about a situation or event. If we think that way, then we realize that nobody can confront your feelings unless you want them to. "If I have a rotten day, that means I allowed it to happen. On the other hand, if I had an awesome day, then I should credit myself for the positivity that reigned in me all day long. I'm the one in charge of myself, what I feel, and how I behave."

Chapter 5: Working on Specifically Anxiety, Negativity, and Stress

Anxiety is a word that is quite common to most people, but funnily enough, not many people can define the word. When you experience a feeling of worry, nervousness, or unease about something, or maybe about the uncertainty of an outcome, then you are anxious.

Anxiety in itself is usually a disorder that affects how we feel or behave. This disorder can even cause some physical symptoms. However, if you are facing such an impairment, you don't have to live with it. Anxiety is treatable.

The best approach to take with the aim of treating is to take on some therapy sessions. Cognitive Behavioral Therapy (CBT), Psychotherapy, and Exposure Therapy are some of the therapies one may majorly consider. The thing with these therapies is that they will help you in controlling your anxiety levels and even help you conquer your fears.

Treating Anxiety Disorders

Some may ask the question: "Why should I go through some hectic therapy session just to treat the disorder while I can simply buy medication and achieve the same result in the comfort of my house?" That can be an excellent way to tackle it, but the problem is that it is only short term. This is because the medication will just eliminate the physical symptoms, leaving behind the underlying causes of your worries and nervousness.

Research has shown that therapy is an effective method to tackle anxiety. How? It simply gives you the tools to overcome your fear and teaches you how to use them.

Therapies are usually considered long-term by most people. However, this is not the case with CBT-based anxiety therapy. Surprisingly, within the first eight to ten months, many people are usually okay. The length of these therapies is generally measured by the severity of the disorder, and also the type. There are various types of anxiety disorders like Generalized Anxiety Disorder (GAD), Obsessive Compulsive Disorder (OCD), Panic Disorder, and many more. It is now also obvious to note that therapy should be tailored to one's specific symptoms. A person suffering from GAD cannot undergo the same therapy session as one suffering from OCD.

As mentioned before, there are various types of anxiety therapies that can be considered. However, the two leading treatments are Cognitive Behavioral Therapy and Exposure Therapy. These therapies can be used alone or be accompanied by other types of treatment. Another thing to note is that these therapies can be done at an individual level or to a group of people who have the same anxiety problems. We are going to cover the CBT part.

Cognitive Behavioral Therapy for Anxiety

Cognitive Behavioral Therapy primarily works to alleviate both negative cognitions, that is, thoughts and beliefs, and also maladaptive behaviors associated with anxiety. CBT seeks to blend the best parts of behavior and cognitive therapies.

As the name suggests, there are two main components to this

therapy: Cognitive Therapy and Behavioral Therapy. Cognitive therapy is the part that involves one's thoughts. This part examines how one's negative thoughts contribute to anxiety. Behavioral treatment, on the other hand, examines one's behavior and reactions when in situations that trigger anxiety. It is important to note that this type of treatment mainly focuses on our thoughts rather than the events. This is because one's thoughts determine one's feelings. Let's take an event, like that of getting a job somewhere you never thought you would ever be employed. This event can lead to various feelings which are determined by how you think about the situation. For example:

- The thought that you are fortunate to have landed in such a job will make you feel thrilled and jovial.

- The thought that you are not qualified enough for such a high-end job may make you feel undeserving of the opportunity, and this can lead to stress.

The above represents the same situation but two very different feelings that can be achieved by merely how you think.

Generally, for people with anxiety disorders, their decisions are often clouded with negative thoughts that lead to negative emotions of worry, nervousness, or fear. For such people, Cognitive Behavioral Therapy usually comes in handy because it helps them identify and fight these negative thoughts, thereby avoiding negative emotions that cause anxiety.

Thought Challenging in CBT

Thought challenging is a useful technique used in CBT that helps one consider situations from multiple angles, using actual evidence from your life. It involves challenging one's negative thoughts and replacing them with more positive and realistic opinions. We covered this in the last chapter.

This technique usually involves three steps. Namely:

1. Identifying Negative Thoughts

Anxiety and negative thoughts are a very evil duo that can lead to very severe problems. People with an anxiety disorder tend to perceive things or events more seriously than other people. For example, a person who fears dogs will consider touching them as life-threatening. Somebody else will view this as safe as long as he or she approaches the dog in a friendly way. This step can be tough to take because identifying one's fear is not that simple. The only thing, however, that one must ask is what feeling you had when you started feeling anxious.

This is the only sure way to determine your fear.

2. Challenging negative thoughts

Once the fears and the negative thoughts have been identified, the next thing is to test these thoughts. What does this mean? It basically means evaluating the negative thoughts. Why do these thoughts occur naturally to you? In this stage, one has to question the evidence behind these negative thoughts and also try to identify any unhelpful beliefs that may lead to negative thoughts. A strategy that one may use in challenging these thoughts is by weighing the advantages and disadvantages of worrying or fearing something.

3. Replacing negative thoughts with positive ones

Once you have challenged these negative thoughts, it is now time to replace these negative thoughts with more realistic and positive thoughts. If this proves hard, one may also find some calming thoughts or words that you can say to yourself if you are facing a situation that causes anxiety.

However, replacing negative thoughts with positive ones is usually easier said than done. This is because the negative thoughts are typically due to a long-term belief which needs much courage and time to break. It is for this reason that cognitive behavioral therapy includes practicing on your own at home.

Managing Stress Self-Help

What is stress? Stress is a state of emotional or mental strain or tension resulting from adverse or demanding circumstances. While in this state, one feels as if there are very many demanding actions that must be taken while the resources needed are minimal. The strain or tension can be caused by many external factors like illness, work, home, or even family environments. Funnily enough, even those events that are considered joyful like holidays can also lead to stress.

Why is managing one's stress helpful? Stress can have a hold on your life, causing you to be sad and thus less productive. It affects your emotional equilibrium and also narrows your ability to think correctly and clearly. Effective stress management can, therefore, go a long way towards relieving a huge burden off your shoulders.

How do you determine whether or not you are under stress? There are various thoughts, emotions, physical sensations, and even behaviors that are associated with this form of mental pressure. Some of these include:

THOUGHTS

- I'll never accomplish this.

- It's not fair. Someone should be helping me.

- This is too much for me.

EMOTIONS

- Angry

- Depressed

- Hopeless

- Impatient

PHYSICAL SENSATIONS

A physical sensation is a physical response to stress and is caused by the body's adrenaline response. Some of the physical feelings associated with stress therefore are:

- Breathing faster

- Hot and sweaty

- Restless

- Bowel problems, usually short pains

- Difficulty in concentrating because one's mind is focused elsewhere

- A headache

BEHAVIOR

- Lack of sleep

- Lack of appetite

- One is not able to settle

- Use of drugs or even an increase in their use. For example, if one is used to smoking, there will be an increased tendency to smoke

Making Positive Changes

This is aimed at basically managing one's stress levels. Various steps can be followed to make positive changes. They include:

1. Identify the sources of stress or the stressors in your life

It's the first step towards making a positive change. This step is not as straightforward as it sounds. Finding the source of chronic stress can be very complicated. To ease things a bit for you, here are some of the questions that you can ask yourself to identify the cause of stress.

- What makes you stressed?

- Where am I when I get stressed?

- What am I doing when I get stressed?

- Who am I with when I get stressed?

- What change can I make?

Some may notice that there is very little that they can do to change some situations. These tiny things could make the difference you need, so do not hesitate to perform them.

2. Identify the factors that keep the problem going

Once you have identified the sources of your stress, it is now time to identify the factors that keep this problem going.

3. Thinking differently

This step is fundamentally mental. It means that all you have to change is your thinking towards various situations. To help you improve your thinking, here are some questions that you ought to ask yourself when faced with a particular case:

- What am I reacting to?

- What is it that is going to happen here?

- Is this fact or opinion?

- How helpful is it for me to think this way?

- Is it even worth it?

- Am I overestimating the threat?

- What meaning am I giving to this situation?

- Is there another way of looking at this?

- What advice would I give to someone else in this situation?

- Can I do things differently here?

Once you have asked yourself these questions and answered them frankly, then you will be able to think positively about a situation.

4. Doing things differently

This step will help with reducing both stress and anxiety. Why? During stress, one usually feels as if many demands cannot be achieved with the available resources. Therefore, doing things differently by maybe considering what applications are most important can help reduce stress levels.

On the other hand, doing things differently can help in reducing anxiety, in that you can now decide to make time for yourself each day to relax or just for fun. One might also choose to create a healthy balance, in that you have time to work, rest, and do other things that concern you.

Tips to Work on Anxiety, Negative Thinking, and Stress

There are several ways of fighting anxiety, negative thinking, and stress:

1. Understand Your Thinking Style

This step right here is the first step to take to change the negative thoughts that one usually has. One must understand how they think precisely. Here are some thinking styles that may help you:

- If you tend to believe that when you fail at one thing, then you have failed at everything, then you are a polarized or black and white thinker.

- If you tend to know what people feel about you and why they act the way they do without them saying so, then you are a person that jumps to conclusions.

- If you tend always to expect disaster to strike no matter what, then you are a catastrophizing thinker. This type of thinker always asks the question: "what if?"

2. The Ability to Recognize Thought Distortions

Once you are able to identify your thinking style, one is able thereby to determine whether it is a thought distortion or not. Types of thought distortions are like those given above in the first step. They include: catastrophizing, making extremely negative predictions, and also making black or white judgments.

3. The Ability to Recognize Rumination

What is rumination? It is a deep or considered thought about something. Typically, when people ruminate, their problem-solving capacity is significantly reduced. Therefore, it is vital for one to recognize this stage during problem-solving and avoid it at all possible costs.

If avoiding ruminating proves to be hard, then the best thing to do when ruminating is to accept that you are having certain thoughts, recognize that they might not be correct, and then allow them to pass in their own mind rather than trying to block them out.

4. Cope with Criticism

Criticism is one thing that cannot be avoided in life. On the other hand, it can also lead to unnecessary worries if not adequately managed. Therefore, one must be able to learn how to cope with criticism. CBT can help one acquire the skills needed to deal with criticism. During the therapy session, try to weigh out if the blame is constructive or not before deciding whether you can use it or shun it away. Always use evidence to your thoughts so that you can make a decision based on factual evidence.

5. Learn the Art of Mindfulness

Mindfulness is a mental state achieved by focusing one's awareness on the present moment' while calmly acknowledging and accepting his or her feelings, thoughts, and bodily sensations. It is mainly associated with meditation.

Learning this art of mindfulness will help you gain control of your thoughts and emotions. This is because the art teaches one to view one's thoughts and feelings as objects floating past you that you can stop, observe, or even let pass you by. We will cover this as we go on.

6. The Ability to Talk to Oneself Kindly about Imperfections and Mistakes

The tendency of speaking to yourself harshly in the case of imperfection has shown to be of no importance. This is because in most cases it leads to rumination, which then leads to vague problem-solving solutions. On the other hand, research has shown that speaking to yourself calmly can increase self-motivation and also make a person feel much better.

7. Avoiding Thought Stopping

Thought stopping is the complete opposite to mindfulness. This is because it is the act of being on the lookout for any negative thoughts whatsoever and forcing them to be eliminated. The problem with this act is that the more you stop these thoughts, the more they will surface during problem-solving. Therefore, avoiding such thoughts and embracing mindfulness is a much better way.

8. Understanding Your Thinking Diary

What are thinking journals? They are tools that can be used to change any negative thoughts. The importance of these thinking diaries is that they help one identify and determine one's negative thinking styles and thus gain a better understanding of how their beliefs affect their emotions. These diaries are essential in a cognitive behavioral treatment plan and must be completed if you want to capture your thoughts. There are more practicals for that before the conclusion.

Chapter 6: Working on Specifically

Anger and Depression

What is anger? It is a strong feeling of annoyance, displeasure, or hostility towards someone or something. Anger usually occurs as a natural response to feeling attacked, frustrated, or even being humiliated. It is human nature to get angry. The fury, therefore, is not a bad feeling per se, because at times it can prove to be very useful. How is this even possible? Anger can open one's mind and help them identify their problems which could drive one to get motivated to make a change which could help in moulding their lives.

When is Anger a Problem?

Anger, as we have just seen, is normal in life. The problem only comes in when one cannot manage their anger, and it causes harm to people around them or even themselves.

How does one notice when their anger is becoming harmful? When one starts expressing anger through unhelpful or destructive behavior, or even when one's mental and physical health starts deteriorating. That's when one knows that the situation is getting out of hand.

It is the way a person behaves that determines whether or not they have problems with their anger. If the way they act affects their life or relationships, then there is a problem, and they should think about getting some support or treatment.

What is Unhelpful Angry Behaviour?

Anger may be familiar to everyone, but people usually express their rage in entirely different ways. How one behaves when they are angry depends on how much control they have over their feelings. People who have less control over their emotions tend to have some unhelpful angry behaviors. These are behaviors that cause damage to themselves or even damage to people or things around them. They include:

Outward Aggression and Violence

This is whereby one directs their anger towards people or things around them. Some of the behaviors here may include shouting at people, fighting people, slamming doors, hitting or throwing things, or being verbally abusive. These types of actions can be very frightening and dangerous to people around, especially children. They can cause severe consequences like the loss of a job or even injuring a loved one or just basically anyone around.

Inward Aggression

This is where one directs their anger towards themselves. Some of the behaviors here may include telling oneself that they hate themselves, denying themselves, or even cutting themselves off the world.

Non-Violent or Passive Aggression

In this case, one does not direct their anger anywhere; rather they stick with the feeling in them. Some of the behaviors here may include ignoring people, refusing to speak to people, refusing to do tasks, or even deliberately doing chores poorly or late. These types of behaviors are usually the worst ways to approach such situations. They may seem less destructive and harmful, but they do not relieve one of the heavy burden that is causing them to be angry.

Preparation

Weigh Your Options

In life, many things may be out of one's control. These things vary from the weather, the past, other people, intrusive thoughts, physical sensations, and one's own emotions. Despite all these, the power to choose is always disposable to any human. Even though one might not be able to control the weather, one can decide whether or not to wear heavy clothing. One can also choose how to respond to other people.

The first step, therefore, in dealing with anger is to recognize a choice.

Steps to Take in Managing Anger

1. A "Should" Rule is Broken

Everybody has some rules and expectations for one's behavior, and also for other people's behavior. Some of these rules include "I should be able to do this", "She should not treat me like this," and, "They should stay out of my way". Unfortunately, no one has control over someone else's actions. Therefore, these rules are always bound to be broken and people may get in one's way. This can result in anger, guilt, and pressure.

It is therefore essential to first break these "should" rules to fight this anger. The first step to make in breaking these rules is to accept the reality of life that someone usually has very little control over other people's lives. The next step is for one to choose a direction based on one's values. How does one know their values? One can identify their values by what angers them, frustrates them, or even enrages them. For example, let's take the rule of "They should stay out of my way". This rule may mean the values of communication, progress, or even cooperation. What do these values mean to someone? Does one have control over them?

Finally, one can act by their values. To help with this, here are two questions one should ask themselves:

- What does one want in the long run?

- What constructive steps can one take in that direction?

2. What Hurts?

The second step is to find the real cause of pain or fear after breaking the rules. These rules usually do not mean the same to one's body. This is because some states of being can hurt one's self-esteem more than others.

To understand this better, let's take the example of Maryah who expects that no one should talk ill of her. Then suddenly Kelvin comes up to her and says all manner of things to her. This, therefore, makes Maryah enraged. In such a scenario, Maryah should ask herself what hurts her. The answer to this question will bring out a general belief about Kelvin and herself. She will think that "Kelvin is rude", "She is powerless", or even that "She is being made the victim". All these thoughts may hurt her. What may even hurt her most is that she has no control over Kelvin's behavior.

Once she has noted that she has no control, she may now consider seeing Kelvin's words as a mere opinion rather than an insult. This will make her not see herself as a victim but as a person just receiving a piece of someone else's mind about herself.

3. Hot Thoughts.

After one has identified what really hurts them, it is now time to identify and most importantly replace the hot, anger-driven and reactive thoughts with more level-headed, more relaxed and reflective thoughts. Here are some fresh ideas that may be of importance to someone:

Hot thought: "How mean can he be!"

Cool thought: "He thinks he is so caring."

Hot thought: "They are stupid!"

Cool thought: "They are just human."

4. Anger

All the above steps, as one may have noticed, relate to the thoughts. This is because one has first to tackle with the ideas before now getting to the emotion. In this step, therefore, one is going to respond to the anger arousal itself. There are three ways that one can follow to respond to this emotion:

- One may indulge in relaxation. This relaxation can come in many forms, like enjoying some music, practising some progressive muscle relaxation like yoga, and also visualization.

- One may also use that feeling to do some constructive work. When one is angry, there is usually a large amount of energy that one uses at that time. This is the reason that when angry, one can break down things that they would never break when calm. Imagine, therefore, how much that energy would do for someone if just directed to some constructive work.

- One may also try to redefine anger when one gets angry. What does this mean? Once a person is angry, one can try to remind themselves of how anger is a problem that fuels aggression and can cause harm to loved ones and even oneself.

5. Moral Disengagement

Moral disengagement is the process of convincing oneself that ethical standards do not apply to themselves in a particular context. In simple words, this step will help one examine the beliefs that turn anger into aggression. These beliefs usually act as mere excuses or justification for destructive acts. Some of these beliefs include "I don't care", "This is the only way I can get my point across", or even "It is high time they recognize me". These beliefs need to be identified early enough and gotten rid of before they can con one into throwing one's morals aside. One sure way of getting rid of them is by reminding oneself of the cost of such beliefs and the advantages of striving for understanding.

6. Aggression

In this step one now needs to examine the behaviors that arise from aggression and try to fight them. Fighting these behaviors can be achieved if one calms down and puts themselves in the other person's shoes. This will help one understand why the other person is acting in such a manner, what they may be feeling, or even what they may be thinking. This approach will help to:

- Decrease the anger for all parties involved.

- Increase the chance of having a reasonable conversation with the parties involved, and thus everybody is heard.

7. Outcome

The final step of this procedure is to reduce resentment towards others, and also guilt towards oneself.

Treating depression with cognitive behavioral therapy.

What is depression? Depression is a feeling of severe despondency and dejection. In life, it is only natural for one to feel less than a hundred per cent at times. This is like when one is battling with a drug addiction or has relationship problems. However, this low feeling sometimes gets a hold of one's life and won't go. This is what we call depression. Depression can make one feel lonely and hopeless.

If one has such feelings, there is light at the end of the tunnel. Cognitive Behavioral Therapy is here to restore one's hope in life. This is because it can help one think more healthily, and also help in overcoming a particular addiction.

Before getting more in-depth with the advantages of CBT on a depressed person, let's first look at the different types of depression.

Types of Depression

Depressions are of various kinds. They can either occur alone or concurrently with an addiction. The best thing, however, is that the following categories are treatable through using CBT.

Major Depression

This type of depression is also called major depressive disorder. This disorder occurs when one feels depressed most of the time for most days of the week. Some of the symptoms associated with this disorder are:

- Weight loss or weight gain

- Being tired often

- Trouble getting sleep

- Thoughts of suicide

- Concentration problems

- Feeling restless or agitated

If one experiences five or more of these symptoms on most days for two weeks or longer, then they have this disorder.

Persistent Depressive Disorder (PDD)

This type of depression usually lasts for two years or even longer. The symptoms associated with disorder include:

- Sleeping too much or too little

- Fatigue

- Low self-esteem

Bipolar Disorder

A person with such a disorder usually experiences mood episodes that range from extremes of high energy with an "up" mood to low periods.

How CBT Helps with Negative Thoughts of Depression

The cognitive behavioral therapy understands that when one has low moods, they tend to have negative thinking. This negative thinking usually brings cases of hopelessness, depression, and can also lead to a change in behavior.

CBT, therefore, works to help with the patterns of behavior that need to be changed. In short, it works to recalibrate the part of the brain that keeps a tight hold on happy thoughts.

Five CBT Techniques to Counteract the Negative Thinking of Depression

There are several techniques that one can follow to help with fighting off negative thoughts. Before starting these steps, one should make sure that they are ready to undertake them and should keep track of themselves. Here are some of the steps:

- **Locate the problem and brainstorm for solutions**

The first step is to discover the cause of the problem. This step requires one to talk with one's inner self. Once the idea of what the problem might be dawns on you, write it down in simple words. Then write down a list of things that one can do to improve the problem.

- **Write self-statements to counteract negative thoughts**

Once the cause of the problem has been discovered, it is now time to identify the negative thoughts that seem to pop up in one's brain every time. Write self-statements to counteract each foul view. These self-statements are statements that are going to stuff up the negative thoughts. One should always recall all their self-statements and repeat them back to themselves every time a negative thought pops up. However, these self-statements should continually be refreshed because they can at times be too routine.

- **Find new opportunities to think positive thoughts**

Michael is a person who always sees the negative part of people before noticing their bright side. These people, more often than not, usually get depressed quickly. To remedy this, they should always change their thinking and think positively. This, for example, in the case of Michael, can be like first noticing and appreciating how neat people are. This type of thinking can be tough to change to. Here are some of the recommended ways that one can adjust to such thinking;

- Set one's phone to remind them to reframe their minds to something positive.

- Pairing up with someone who is working on this same technique. This will make one have positive thoughts, and also get to enjoy them with someone else.

- **Finish each day by visualizing its best parts**

After each day, one can write down the most exciting events of the day and try to remember them. Sharing such moments online can even help one form new associations, and also thinking ways that can prove to be very helpful.

- **Learn to accept disappointment as a normal part of life**

In life, disappointment is bound to come one's way. How one deals or behaves after a disappointing event determines how fast one is going to move forward. Take for example John who just lost a job interview. This is a thing that can happen to anyone. The way he responds to this situation will determine how fast he is going to move forward. If he starts getting the thoughts of "I am a failure", "The world is so unfair to me", or even "I will never succeed in life", then he is moving in the wrong direction. The best way to approach this situation is by allowing himself to be disappointed and remembering that he had no control over the situation. Later, he can write some things he has learnt from the experience and things he can do to remedy it next time.

Conclusion

In conclusion, anger and depression are a duo that can affect one's life negatively if not adequately managed. The best way to handle these two feelings is by undergoing a CBT that will help one learn new ways of thinking, which may help one change how they perceive things in life. This can make one view events in a different way for the better. It is also important to note that one usually does not have control over everything in their lives. Some things are just not in one's hands.

CBT, therefore, teaches one how to deal with such situations before they can get the better of someone.

Chapter 7: Deleting BAD Habits and Creating New POSITIVE Ones

Evaluating your thoughts and ideas as the most relevant step of cognitive behavior therapy (CBT)

Killing Subconscious and Conscious Habits

Having a sense of what CBT entails and how useful your thoughts impact different moods and perceptions, you can now move to the one and the most critical first steps of learning how to identify negative thoughts and energy around you.

Why is it Hard to Stick to Good Habits?

We often fell into harmful habits including:

- Smoking

- Stress and junk eating

- Fighting

- Having a boring career

- Watching TV all day

- Stalking someone

But why? Is it always a struggle to change your unhealthy behaviors? Whenever you get inspired to create a change, you find yourself doing the same thing rather than something more desirable? This is because we usually try to implement changes using the wrong method. In this chapter, I will guide you through how to integrate both real-life experiences and science as a way of changing your unhealthy habits for the rest of your life. If you can change your thoughts, you can change your habits.

Differentiate Between Bad Habits and Addictions

It is easy to ignore harmful practices such as smoking to be a small innocent routine that "sometimes" gets out of hand. However, your friends and relatives view it differently; maybe they perceive it to be a developing hidden addiction that needs urgent action.

Remember, not all habits are breakable; you can only change certain habits when you follow this guide. Habits recognized as addictive will require you involve professional counselling, join a support group, or use this self-help book to solve it if you can by yourself.

Are you an addict? Here is the list of questions to ask yourself:

Do you:

- Have financial troubles as a result of spending almost all your income on the activity?

- Endure withdrawal symptoms whenever you stop the

habit? (anger, frustration, restlessness)

- Have health complications affiliated to the activity?

- Prefer this activity to other enjoyable activities?

- Hide or refuse to acknowledge your behavior from people?

- Allow the activity to interfere with your normal routine?

- Seek binges whenever you are on the habit?

- Save extra supplies for emergencies (hiding cans of beer in your bedroom)

- Have trouble balanced your limits on the activity? For instance, one shot of liquor leads you to binge drink the whole bottle to blackout.

- Engage in the activity to deal with emotional and stress problems?

- Participate in dangerous behavior whenever doing the activity?

- Destroy your interpersonal relationship because of this activity?

Some or all of these symptoms are usually experienced by people who languish on alcoholism, binge eating, drug abuse, and smoking. However, it is recommended to seek a professional physician to examine your possible addiction. Here are a few suggestions on ways to go about it other than self-help:

- Visit a psychologist or behavioral therapist who deals

with habits.

- Be a member of a group like NA (narcotics anonymous) or support group.

- Join a promising weight-loss group that provides long-term life changes rather than fad diets.

- Ask your physician for a different non-addictive way to conquer cravings.

Don't hold back to ask help from others, since some addictions can't be overcome by following a simple checklist. If you think you are experiencing troubles with your addiction, then get assistance.

The Science behind Your Habits

(The 3 Rs of habit change)

This is a simple 3-step loop that every habit follows:

- Reminder (what induces the behavior)

- Routine (the activity itself)

- Reward (an advantage you get from doing the action)

This pattern has been approved again and again by behavioral psychology researchers. Let's see how 3 R's works, in reality, using the case of smoking a cigarette.

- ***Step one:*** You smell a cigarette from a distance (reminder). It initiates the behavior. The smells trigger your mind to smoke.

- **Step two:** You smoke (routine). The actual habit. Whenever you detect the smell of a cigarette, you have a habit of smoking one or more.

- **Step three:** You get stimulated (reward). The benefit gained after smoking. In this case, the reward was getting relaxed and contented from the cigarette smoking.

- **Results:** In the case where the reward is positive, then the pattern returns a positive result which tells the brain, "the next time you smell a cigarette, smoke one."

How Can You Create New Habits and Stick to Them?

Here's how:

Creating new positive and productive habits based on the old ones that will make you happy and distract you from the negative emotions.

Step 1: Use a Prevailing Habit as a Reminder for Your New Ones

Friends will tell you that to initiate a new pattern you require to practice self-control, but some of us would tend to disagree. Trying to remember and getting motivated is not a useful way of using CBT. To be motivated is an off and on feeling, right? Therefore, you can't rely on something that changes (motivation) to create something that you want to be regular (new habit).

85

For this reason, a reminder is such an essential part in creating a new routine. A definite reminder encourages you to initiate your new habit by concealing your new behavior in something that you are currently doing, instead of depending on getting motivated.

For instance, I created a new habit of praying every day before going to bed. The act of going to bed was something that I already did, and it triggers my new behavior. To prevent myself from having to remember to pray, I placed my Bible on the bedside drawer. Whenever I am off to bed the bible will trigger my new habit of praying. A visible reminder like the Bible links the new practice with the ongoing behavior, therefore making it easier to change.

How to Determine Your Reminder

Sticking with your new habit requires you to set up a system that simplifies your start. However, selecting the right reminder for your new habits is the essential step to making change effortless. The reminder should be unique to your life and new pattern you are creating. The best way to find a great reminder for your new habit is to write two lists. The first list contains the things that you do every day without fail. For example:

- Take a shower

- Brush your teeth

- Dress

- Take breakfast

- Go to work

- Sit down for dinner

- Get into bed

Most of this activity is carried out daily and can act as reminders for new habits. For example, after taking breakfast, you immediately go to work.

In the second list, note down things that occur to you each day:

- Your alarm rings

- You get an email

- Your doorbell rings

- A song ends

- The sun sets

These events, when used effectively, can act as triggers for your new habit. For instance, whenever your alarm rings you wake up for work. In the case where you want to be happier, using the list above you can choose a reminder "taking breakfast" and use it to say one thing that you are anticipating and delighted to do for the rest of the day.

Step 2: Make Your Habits Easy to Start

Earlier in this guide, I mentioned how easy it is to get caught up in the desire to create a massive change in your life. We see a fantastic weight loss transformation and anticipate that we need to lose 20 pounds in the next month.

I've experienced the same, so I get it and understand your enthusiasm. I appreciate that you are willing to make a change for the greater good of your life, and I will do what I can to help you accomplish that transformation. It is critical to remember that permanent change starts with small steps of your daily habits, not once in a lifetime transformations.

If you want to start a new healthier habit, then you need to start small. It is said, "Make it so easy that you can't say no". At first, performance doesn't matter. Alternatively what matters is becoming that person who adheres to their new habit- regardless of how small or irrelevant it seems. You can then develop to the level of performance that you desire when your behavior becomes a habit.

Homework: Decide on a new habit you want to start then ask yourself, "How can I make it so easy to do that I can't say no to it?"

Step 3: Reward Yourself

Negative thoughts, anxiety, and depression make us feel bad about ourselves, but we always thrive to continue doing things that create happiness and joy in our hearts. In the case of sticking to new habits, it is important to reward yourself each time you exercise the new habit.

For example, if I'm working to achieve a fit body, then I will regularly tell myself after a workout, "that was a good workout" or, "nice job; you have shed a few calories today."

You could even go the extra mile if you feel like it and tell yourself, "victory" or," excellent" each time you perform your new habit.

"I have done it myself, and I can attest that it is an incredible way of rewarding oneself."

- Pray before going to bed. "success."

- Eat a balanced diet meal. "excellent."

- Go for a morning jog. "superb."

- Clean my room. "Good work."

If you aren't someone who generally does positive self-talk as a way of rewarding yourself, you can get used to it suddenly. No matter how silly it sounds, research has proven that paying yourself a compliment is a vital component of developing your habit. Reward yourself with some credit and celebrate every small achievement.

Consequently, ascertain that the new developing habits that you are expanding are meaningful to you. It will be tough to reward yourself for something that you are only doing to impress others or you think you will get approval from it. Create new habits that you are interested in and familiar with because it is your life, not your friend's or relative's life. Make sure you spend your time on things that are crucial to you specifically.

Step 4: Establish Your Target Goal

Getting rid of bad habits is similar to setting a goal. However, you can't develop new habits without having a clear outcome in mind and with an exact target date. It is essential to appreciate the process of setting goals, finding obstacles, and then adjusting your behaviors to reach those goals.

For example, you can't just say, "I want to lose a few pounds." Instead, you need to find a gym to sign in and have a personal trainer guide you on what to eat and which exercise to do, and the date you will start this journey.

The following would be an excellent goal: "Starting June 3rd, I will no longer sleep past 7 o'clock. Instead, I will wake up, take a healthy breakfast, go for a morning jog, and afterwards attend my gym routine with my trainer." You notice this result has a deadline with a specific outcome. By 3rd June, you will know if the routine is working or not. That's how simple it is to set a goal that will break your bad habits.

Comparatively, since we are stressing a one-month trial period, I propose you create some array of metrics for the end of 30 days. Upon that stated date, you can choose either to continue with the new habit change.

Conclusion

Indeed, cognitive behavioral therapy is useful in evaluating your thoughts that otherwise influence your perceptions and moods. Your brain needs to be trained to identify the difference between bad habits and good ones. This may take longer and require patience, so set a goal and follow the above steps so that you can achieve a long-term change.

Chapter 8: Goal Setting and Time Management

Goal Setting

What is a goal? A goal is the ultimate thing that you would want to do at the end of the treatment or therapy. Goal setting should be very precise and to the point if it is to help someone. What does this mean? For example, instead of just saying that at the end of the program, you would like to feel "less depressed" or even feel "better", one should ask oneself the things that make them "less depressed" or even those that make them feel happy. These things are what one should set as their goals. Some of these things may include:

- To go out and travel or even visit somewhere.

- To get and enjoy a movie with someone.

- To quietly enjoy a good cup of coffee.

These goals can be very enticing to write and thus one may end up with a lot of goals. This should always be avoided because a lot of goals can be very confusing. One should work with about one to three goals. These goals, however, should be reviewed often because they can become too common.

Setting a Goal

This book is aimed at the self-help of the reader. For any self-help to be effective, one should set some goals. These goals should be SMART. What does SMART mean? These goals should be Specific, Measurable, Achievable, Relevant, and lastly, Time limited.

Here are some tips that may be of help when setting a goal:

- Ask yourself what you want to be able to do.

- Be as specific as you can by stating how often you want to do something.

- Set realistic goals.

- State the problems positively. This is by starting them with "to be able to" instead of "to stop".

- Ask someone you know well and trust to help you.

Why are self-help goals usually important? Self-help goals usually help to guide a person. Not having these goals is like finding directions to a place which you didn't want to go to. Apart from goals, one must also identify their triggers. What are triggers? Triggers are situations that cause anxiety or even low moods. One should fight to eliminate these.

Triggers from Self-help

Here are some tips that may help you with this:

- Identify what triggers your anxiety or low mood.

- Look at your own Hot Cross Bun.

- Identify what needs to change for you to feel better.

Goals from Self-Help

Here are some tips that may help with this:

- What do you hope to gain?

- What do you hope to have achieved?

- What will be different for you?

Remember that the goals must be as SMART as possible.

Common Obstacles That You May Face

While trying to reach these self-help goals, one might come across some challenges. These include;

- Worries about getting things 'right' may lead to people not completing these tasks.

- Being very busy and not prioritizing the content and techniques contained in this book.

- Feeling low or unmotivated may make it seem more difficult to do the work.

What do you think could prevent you from being able to achieve these goals?

What could you do to ensure that these obstacles do not prevent you from achieving your goals and overcoming your problems?

Time Management

What is time management? Time management is the ability to use one's time effectively or productively, especially in the workplace. Time management is a skill that involves prioritizing activities and focusing one's resources on the most important one's while eliminating the time wasters and disruptions. Therefore, time management is a skill that involves intense decision making, either large or small, that changes the shape of one's life.

In life no one usually has control of a day's events. Anything is bound to happen. However, one usually has some control over what they can do. This is the power of time management. Even in the cases of structured times, one is able to choose and prioritize activities that they are going to undertake. It is through the exercise of these choices that one has control over their time.

Planning and organizing are two secrets of time management that one must know. For effective time management, one must plan their time in a way that harmonizes with their unique requirements, inclinations, and interests. The goal of time management is usually to eliminate any time wasters. It is important to note, therefore, that even the saving of five minutes in one's schedule can go a long way towards improving one's life by increasing their productivity.

Time management usually begins with an assessment of one's time usage, followed by coming up with a schedule on how to carry out different activities in respect to the time.

Seven Basic Skills to Improve Your Productivity

1. Get Started

For one to improve their productivity, one has to get started on a particular task. Getting the motivation to start is usually a very hard task. In life, the differences between successful people and the others is that they are willing to perform a task. They are always ready. Therefore, it is important for one to bite their own bullet and get down to the tasks at hand.

Most are the times when it is difficult to find self-motivation. In cases like these, one should work out the obstacles and get rid of them – may it be practical or even psychological obstacles.

2. Make it Part of Your Routine

Routines usually create a reassuring framework for each and every day that tasks will be completed. This therefore reduces the hustle of determining what activities to carry out. So, one should create and allocate tasks with time slots and later let the routine guide you through the day.

3. Do not Say YES, when You Want to Say NO

For one to improve their productivity, confidence and self-esteem are two important things to have. It is sometimes difficult to resist the demands of other people, especially friends. This is especially when one is feeling depressed or has lost sight of the important things.

So, keep in mind that every yes that you say, is usually a no to something else. Therefore, it is important for one to find the other thing that is going to be hindered by a yes and try to consider if you can take away time from it.

4. Distant Elephants

Normally, elephants look very small when far away as opposed to when they are near. Therefore, one should always deal with important tasks and not commit themselves to unimportant activities, no matter how far they are.

5. Break it Down

One should break down tasks into smaller realistic and achievable tasks. Large tasks are usually very overwhelming and can cause depression or even anxiety. On the other hand, smaller tasks are usually less overwhelming and, upon completion of each task, one usually has some sense of satisfaction and achievement that fuels them on to the next task.

6. Beware of Perfectionism

Perfectionism is considered to be a very close companion of procrastination. Therefore, for one to increase their productivity, one should not consider how perfectly a task is done. One should only aim at achieving the target. When one aims at the target only, one may even achieve more than expected.

7. Make a Plan

One should then allocate tasks with some time slots in a routine. A few minutes spent making the routine will save hours which could be otherwise wasted.

Cognitive Behavioral Therapy on Goal

Setting and Time Management

CBT helps one in understanding their body cycles. By working with the body cycles, one can maximize their efficiency which is the ultimate goal of time management. How then does one maximize their efficiency by working with their body cycles? Here is a routine that might come in handy:

Cognitive Tasks 6am-8am.

Cognitive tasks are usually carried out in the morning, when the brain is fresh. These tasks may include problem solving or even calculating. They are usually mental tasks.

Short Term Memory 8am-10am.

These tasks may include the last-minute revision for a test.

Long Term Memory 10am-12pm.

These tasks may include going through and memorizing a speech to be given. These tasks are best performed in the afternoon.

Manual Dexterity 2pm-6pm.

Manual dexterity is the ability of someone to use their hands to perform a difficult action skillfully and with ease. These tasks include physical workouts and keyboarding. These activities are best carried out in the early evenings. This is because muscle coordination is at its peak.

Monitor and Reward Behavior

One should always have the habit of acknowledging what they have already achieved rather than that which has not been accomplished. This is very important because it gives one the motivation to take on other tasks. One should also have the habit of rewarding themselves or even taking a break after achieving a particular task.

Personal Time Management Tool

Time Flies Worksheet

When undergoing the CBT training, one should always have such a worksheet. Here, we can call it a timetable. This worksheet helps you determine where you may have some free time. This is after evaluating all your activities. Then one can see how they can improve their schedule.

Understanding Your Results

As one tries to improve their schedule, one should also consider the effects of their choices on their personal health, and also their well-being. One should not squeeze their schedules in a way that there are no breaks for refreshments or even recreation.

Most people usually just manage around 60 hours of productivity each week. If one's result is above this, then one might need to cut back on either work or school. On the other hand, if one's productivity is below 60 hours, then one should be able to balance the demands of the activities, may it be in school or in the workplace.

Causes of Time Wastage

Here are some reasons that can lead to time wastage in someone's life.

1. Lack of Proper Planning.

Some people fail to see the benefit of planning their activities. This is maybe the main reason why they do not achieve a lot of tasks, because there is time being wasted somewhere.

To remedy this, therefore, one should recognize that planning takes time but saves time in the long run.

2. Lack of Priorities.

Lack of priorities is usually brought about when one does not have goals in life. Therefore, to remedy this, one must set some goals and objectives which will drive you.

3. Over-Commitment.

Over commitment can also lead to time wastage. Over-commitment is usually caused by factors like broad interests and the lack of prioritizing these interests. The solution to this, therefore, is abandoning some interests and then deciding which will come first amongst those that remain.

4. Management by Crisis.

Management crisis is usually caused by unrealistic time estimates. One should therefore allow for adequate time, and also be opportunity-oriented so as to remedy this.

5. Haste.

Haste is usually caused by:

- Impatience with detail or routine matters.

- Lack of planning ahead.

- Attempting too much in too little time.

This problem however can be remedied by distinguishing between urgent and important, taking time to plan, attempting less, or maybe taking time to do it right the first time.

6. Visitors.

Visitors are usually brought about by either enjoyment of socializing or maybe the inability to say no. This therefore can be remedied by saying no, doing it elsewhere, or even saying that you are not available.

7. Indecision.

Indecision is usually caused by lack of confidence in the facts or even fear of the consequence of a mistake. This can be remedied by improving fact finding and validating procedures, accepting that risks are inevitable, and also maybe using mistakes as a learning process.

Chapter 9: Other Ways to Support Psychological Health

Apart from using CBT, there are other ways to support psychological and overall mental health. We all recognize the importance of mental health but the main question here is how do we go about achieving it? Possible conditions that compromise proper mental ability include either being born with the defect or having acquired it in the process due to stress, depression, or substance abuse. In the case of it being a birth defect, this book will not help the patient since that is beyond human control. On the other hand, if you acquired it through one of the mentioned ways or similar ones, then keep on reading and thank you for reading this far.

What is Mental Health?

According to WHO (World Health Organization), health, which includes mental health, involves a state of entire mental, physical, and social well-being, which means it's not just about the absence of a disease or condition.

The same definition applies to proper mental health, which implies it's not just about the presence or absence of mental disorders such as anxiety and depression, or bipolar disorders, amongst others. If one is mentally healthy, then it means they are aware of their own capabilities, can cope with life's normal dramas, and will work effectively in a bid to make a mark on his or her community.

We can therefore say that good mental health is the core to the effectiveness of an individual and the community around him or her.

In the Name of Good Mental Health

CBT has done a great job in making people realize themselves and be able to get back on track. It has been used to treat several conditions (you can refer to the Introduction to see what CBT can be used to address).

On the other hand, mental health involves more than one strategy if we need to make sure that positivity stays in us on a long-term basis. Promoting good mental health involves utilizing strategies and prepared programs that generate an enabling environment that has the right living conditions for people to abide by and be able to maintain healthy conditions.

There is no particular program aimed at mental health, and that is why it will involve more than CBT.

The range of programs available should be thanked by those who have benefited, since one specific measure may not suit your troubled neighbor. They all give us a chance to enjoy the fruits of staying positive by allowing the mind to adjust the way it thinks.

What Determines Your State of Mental Health?

Mental health has a range of factors that influence it, which is the same as physical health. The factors are also interactive, and they include psychological, biological, and social aspects. Research has shown that the evidence is well portrayed in poverty, low or improper education, low income earning, or poor housing and sanitation.

The declining socioeconomic status that has more disadvantages will force individuals to succumb to mental disorders. Those who are more vulnerable involve the less fortunate or disadvantaged and within a community prone to mental disorders. If other additional factors such as insecurity, hopelessness, poor body health, increased risks of violence and rapid social change are also around, that also partially explains why we may be having improper mental health.

Ways that You can use to Promote Overall Psychological Wellbeing

Here are some things to consider as you look forward to reinstating good mental health.

Look for What is Affecting You

Since we aren't the same, it is crucial that you investigate your individual causes of ill mental health. On the other hand, some shared causes may be becoming stressed, or depressed, finding difficulty to cope or quit something, or generally upset.

There are life events that may affect our mental health. They include:

- Being lonely

- Loss of someone close to you

- Illicit relationships

- Financial issues

- Work related problems

NB: loneliness, insomnia stress and inactivity are all forms of negativity when it comes to mental wellbeing.

At times, it is almost impossible to determine why we experience mental disorders. While it is a cause to worry, there are other factors that will lead to such feelings. They maybe happened or occurred in the past.

They may involve the following:

- Neglect, child abuse, or violence

- Homelessness, especially for those who have experienced foster care

- Social discrimination

- Terminal illness in us or in the family

- Loss of a job or unemployment

- Poverty and debt

- Trauma associated with life experiences such as high-level crime, military issues or being involved in major tragedies such as bomb attacks

Regardless of the cause, what you need to remember is that you have a right to feel great and there is a protocol for you to achieve that.

Building Relationships That Can Help You

Getting involved in social groups or having a friend will give you a sense of belonging if it's not yet there. It will help you cope with difficulty if you manage to do the following:

- ***Connect with loved ones***: Always keep in touch with your friends and relatives with the convenient method available. You can plan to visit, call them, or leave them messages.

- ***Joining social groups:*** What do you like to do? Some of us like playing instruments, others drawing, swimming, and the list is endless.

- ***Talk about your feelings:*** If you have someone that you can trust with your personal issues, it's a good idea to open up to them. It also shows that you are aware of what is happening to you, so explaining it to someone actually helps. At times, it is hard to explain it to our friends, but you can do that to a person who has a similar experience. If you have a chance, please utilize it. There are online groups that one can join to express and try to solve mental matters.

Make Time for Yourself

It can appear selfish to set time for yourself, but it is vital to your overall wellbeing and can help you spring out from mental difficulty.

Mindfulness: Having your presence helps you to realize oneself and be able to manage what we feel. The goal here is to enjoy life again and accept what is around you. We will cover this in detail in the next chapter.

Acquire a new skill: If you learn something that you have been longing for, or will help you later, it gives you the confidence and the joy of achievement. You could sign up for a class or try a new language. Whatever it is, it doesn't have to be big.

Relaxing techniques: Do something that soothes your mind such as having a bath, listening to music, or going for a jog. All these and more will help you cope with stress and mental disorders.

Examine Your Mental Health Status

If you are already aware of your mental condition or difficulty, take the appropriate steps to make sure that you are improving.

- *Talk about what will help you:* If there is a strategy that worked on you before, tell the one helping you out. Let those close to you know what can support you better such as listening to your troubles or making you aware of your issues.

- ***Stay alert for warning signs***: If you can be aware of how you feel and are able to spot signs that depict you are unwell, that is much better. Being aware of such signs will help you when it becomes hectic, and it will also form the base guidance to those who are directing and supporting you.

- ***Use a mood diary:*** Just like we track our day activities, we can also record our moods, and we have seen that is possible in the previous chapters. Have a way to record your moods, the negative issues that you think of, and ways to help you stay positive. If you have no idea how to write one, there are online sources to help you with that such as moodscope.com

- ***Upgrade your self-esteem:*** It is one of the major steps in making yourself ready to challenge your mental issues.

Physical Health is Vital to Mental Wellbeing

Look after your body and what you are subjecting it to. Here are a few recommended things:

Eating Healthy

- Invest in a good balanced diet

- Eat regularly so that your energy levels are constant, and the body can regulate sugar levels

- Have fruits and vegetables aplenty

- Avoid alcohol and other drugs that ruin mental ability

Moving It

Engage in exercise to keep the juices flowing, which will also help you get rid of negativity. Some activities include:

- A walk

- Bike riding

- Swimming

- Yoga

- Football

- Martial arts

- Etc.

Have Enough Sleep

- Tiredness brings in more worry and stress. Doctors' orders direct you to sleep 8 hours per day.

- Have a bedtime routine, such as drinking milk or hot water before sleeping. Later, you can read a book or listen to music that helps you sleep.

- Sleep and wake up at the same time every day.

- Do not drink anything caffeinated after lunch.

As we wrap up this chapter, it is important to consider other methods that will help you gain better mental health as you continue with CBT. That way, you will have more tolls to conquer what you need to get rid of.

Chapter 10: Maintaining Mindfulness

What does the term mindfulness mean? Mindfulness is the quality or state of being conscious or aware of something. Mindfulness is a quality that everyone usually has. It is a quality that is always present to us in every moment. One only gets to realize it if you can take time to appreciate it. By practicing mindfulness, one also practices the art of creating space for ourselves and our reactions.

How can Mindfulness Help One in Overcoming their Challenges?

Mindfulness can be of importance in overcoming your challenges in that:

1. Mindfulness Gives One Perspective.

In times of anger, mindfulness can come in handy by giving you the ability to view a particular situation with a different perspective. One is therefore able to take a step back and make a sane decision devoid of any emotional judgment.

2. Mindfulness Leads You to Acceptance.

Many are the times when one wishes they could change a difficult situation they are maybe going through. This, however, is usually not possible. Mindfulness, in such a case, will teach you how to accept the outcome. It will also teach you that you may lack the power to change the circumstance, but you have all the power to change your attitude toward the circumstance.

3. Mindfulness Helps You Process Anger.

Often are the times in life when unfair circumstances are out of our control. This can cause anger which can lead to destruction of a lot of things in one's life. Mindfulness in this case will help one to understand their anger, rather than just express it. It will also teach one to respond to situations rather than just reacting to them.

4. Mindfulness Gives You Clarity.

This clarity is usually as a result of the perspective that mindfulness gives you. This is because when one removes the emotional judgment when dealing with a situation, one is able to have a clear view of what really happened. This, therefore, allows one to make informed and clear decisions on what to do next.

5. Mindfulness Helps You to Take Care of Yourself.

Mindfulness, as you may have noticed, involves meditation. It is this meditation that helps one understand their body's needs. Therefore, when one is faced with a particular situation, one is able to listen and act in accordance to their body's needs, and this leads to a self-care routine.

How Does One Maintain their Mindfulness?

Some people may find the art of mindfulness hard to comprehend. However, it is a very simple art that one can understand and maintain. Here are some tips that may help you maintain your mindfulness:

1. Practice Mindfulness during Routine Activities.

This tip might not seem that important to most people. However, it is one of the most helpful ways. On a daily basis, most people do not really put much concern on the daily routine activities that they undertake. These activities may include bathing, brushing teeth, or even taking breakfast. Bringing awareness, however, to these activities can help one maintain their mindfulness.

For example, one may try and focus on the way they breathe, their sight, or even their sense of smell. This can make one realize how these routine activities are fun.

2. Practice Right when You Wake up.

Practicing mindfulness early in the morning can be of much importance. This is because it sets one's nervous system for the rest of the day, and thus increases the chances of other mindful moments within the day.

If one finds it hard to practice mindfulness just after waking up, one should try it after having their breakfast.

3. Let Your Mind Wander.

Being 'busy' mentally is usually an asset to any human. This is because a human brain and mind are designed in such a way that they keep on roaming around. These beneficial brain changes are usually attributed to the act of noticing that your mind has wandered, and then non-judgmentally bringing it back. This act of noticing is usually the act of mindfulness.

4. Keep it Short.

Mindfulness is an act that should be practiced several times a day rather than just setting aside a lengthy session in a day. This is because the human brain responds better to bursts of mindfulness rather than a single lengthy session.

For example, occasionally in a day, one can tune their body to focus on maybe how their clothes feel on their body in that moment, or even how they breathe at that moment.

5. Practice Mindfulness while You Wait.

Waiting is one of the common things that makes most people frustrated. Being kept at the reception of an office for almost an hour or even being stuck in traffic in not an experience anybody likes to have. Waiting, however, can be of much importance when one sees it as an opportunity to practice mindfulness.

For example, while stuck in traffic, one can focus on maybe how the movement of the cars is happening or even focus on how the shoes feel on their feet.

6. Pick a Prompt to Remind You to be Mindful.

It is usually human nature to forget. It is only normal, therefore, for one to rely on something that reminds them of something. In this case one can choose any routine activity that will help you to be mindful. This activity can be maybe drinking coffee.

7. Learn to Meditate.

Meditation is usually taken to be like the language to mindfulness. Normally, one has first to learn the language before they can speak the language. It is in the same manner that one has first to learn how to meditate in order to cultivate one's mindfulness skills. Meditation helps one tap into mindfulness with ease.

In conclusion, mindfulness is not a luxury in life. It is an art that helps one improve their brain's focus, and thus reduce their stress in life. This in the end leads to a better self.

Killing Procrastination

Are you fond of avoiding or putting off tasks? Does this action dispute with your true values and beliefs? It is high time you step back and ask yourself authentic questions. How responsible are you to accomplish the tasks in the course of time (or not)? If it is not practical to abide with it then ask yourself what else you can pull off to transform your life's situations in order to avoid executing the same task later.

Do you still find yourself procrastinating certain work that is harmonious with your real values and is essential to achieve your goals? These are the task that requires your energy and positive attitude of learning how to finish it more efficiently and within the deadline. Here is a guide on how you can accomplish your task in your best interest without procrastinating.

1. Stop Worrying

If you take a pause you will notice that we spend most of our time worrying about what is required of us to do instead of focusing our time on actually performing the task that needs to be done. Considerably, it is possible that if we redirected time wasted on worrying and thinking about the task and invest it in more useful manner, you will realize you are almost finishing your task(s).

Usually, this is easier said than done. Firstly, start this process by use of consciousness to acknowledge the times in any given moment when you discover yourself full of worry and rumination. When you discover this, use this incident as a chance to remind yourself to convert your energy in a proper creative manner.

2. Start Small

Once you start working on your task you actually realize it is less demanding than they appear to be. When you are faced with huge workloads or obstacles you can decide to break down tasks into smaller categories and assigning a deadline for each task group. This is an effective and efficient way to carry out your tasks in order to accomplish them on time.

If your desk is stuck with a pile of papers and reports, it is easy to glimpse at it and become overpowered by its absolute weight. Preferably, look at the pile of papers for literally what it is (one simple sheet of paper on top of another sheet). By doing this you will be able to take things to step by step, and at the end you realize you have accomplished a great deal within a short time.

3. Save the Cost of Wasting Time

Do you know the more time you waste on avoiding something uninteresting, troublesome, and repulsive, the more it will cost you later to perform the same task? No matter how much you evade a task it rarely vanishes on its own. It will calmly wait for you to work on it, and during the procrastination period, it is possible that it has piled up into some vulgar appendage for you pull off.

Let's take this example: take out a clean sheet of paper and subdivide it into two columns. Under the first column write down a list of all the irresistible reasons to perform the task (rewards and benefits). Under the second column make a list of all possible reasons to not to do the work (they are the benefits you believe to achieve by avoiding the task). Have a look at the two columns. Which do you see is longer and more reasonable? It is likely that the most effective choice is to take care of the task now rather than later.

4. Challenge Negative Beliefs

It is a common thing for cognitive distortions to get in the way and obstruct the completion of unsatisfactory tasks within the deadline. Start by discovering and observing your own thoughts with better care and clarity. Do you notice what messages you might be sending yourself via a habitual loop of thinking?

Using CBT, begin to rethink your thoughts and identify negative thoughts. Consider them merely for what they are (just thoughts). Thoughts are just created words and pictures that run through your mind. They will bear meaning if you assign them one. Challenge your ridiculous and negative values and question the soundness of your thoughts with absolute apprehensive knowledge. The moment you start thinking positively you reap more benefits.

5. Search for Hidden Rewards

Identify the expected rewards and benefits you will achieve upon accomplishing (and not finishing) the undesirable task that you may have left without notice. What is the short-term and permanently secondary gains that you can anticipate after completing or not completing the task? For instance, a few people procrastinate due to subliminal fear of failure, or because they are such perfectionists. On the other hand, consider how deciding to finish the task will adversely result in reducing anxiety and stress.

Obstacles to Mindfulness and How to Conquer Them

Our current life presents itself daily with different challenges which are not easy, but at times it is highly rewarding. The best way to move forward from one point to the next is to understand the possible troubles and problems and plan a strategy in advance on how you will overcome them. The following ways show how you can overcome your mindfulness obstacles.

1. Mindfulness is a Continuous Effort

Mindfulness takes a lot of effort, but the longer you are persistent the simpler it gets and the more appreciating your life turns. At the very beginning, your thoughts are full of confusion and every little thing seems more challenging. Being in that situation you end up feeling defenseless and trapped, yet when you focus your attention on being who you really are, the easier it becomes to achieve a peaceful mind.

Throughout your day it is important to practice mindfulness. Don't just wait until you sit down so that you can meditate. Concentrate on being aware of your thoughts when you are carrying out your daily routine and it will be obvious to stay mindful when stuff gets tough.

2. Be Aware of Distractions

The journey of becoming mindful is not a smooth road. It appears to be as if the world is throwing problems at you just to challenge your mind. The distractions could be anything from your daily problems, relationship drama, or negative beliefs.

It is best to practice self and mind awareness when you are still young. The more you conquer these obstacles you become better, stronger, and more aware of yourself. Your friends, teachers, and parents are a few people that are supposed to help you discover who you truly are.

3. Progress Takes Time

Progress may appear to be extremely slow. Several times you may find yourself stuck to situations and stuff that you are interested in, which later may not be present. It is unthinkable to be mindful when you are engrossed in the future or still stuck in the past.

Admittedly we all find ourselves in that situation. The more you want something, the more you are obsessing on not having it and desire to have it. Once you start appreciating and become grateful for what you have now, you will realize your life drifting.

4. The Urge to Give up

Like any other journey, the urge to give up may pursue you now and then. During this time, you will be frustrated and almost give up. The world presents itself with similar seasons of cold, heat, and longer winters which come and go. The same thing applies to our life, and when you notice that, the challenging times are there to provide guidance and help you grow, and you will eventually feel relaxed and peaceful.

5. *Don't Forget that the Journey is the Destination*

Have ever realized upon reaching a destination it is not as breathtaking as you thought it would be? Most people forget the fact that the reward of a journey is the journey itself. It is a great joy to accomplish your goals, but it will be devastating if you don't replace that goal with another one. Human beings are dreamers and we all work towards achieving certain goals in our life. People around the world need goals so that they can have a sense of purpose and achievement. It is through the journey that we learn, grow, and transform into a better person. Whenever you exercise mindfulness remember there isn't a final destination, and rather focus on the current happenings and the rest will sort itself.

6. *Don't Run from Your Problems*

Will you be surprised to notice, no matter how enlightened on earth you are, you will still face difficult times and confusing thoughts? The difference is how you are willing to accept the moments for what they really are. When you are able to accept the difficult situation, you will be the protector of your inner space, and it is the only way to guarantee peace of mind.

7. *Your Goals may Question Your Mindfulness*

Setting goals is desirable and efficient for your journey, but when you become attached to them, something undesirable happens. When you are too invested in achieving your goal, you will start feeling frustrated, pissed, and negative.

Attachment disorients our clarity. Many times, you are working towards your goals with the hope of achieving happiness. Do not allow your goals to pull you into a stressful state of mind. If you concentrate on the good things around you, you will gain more happiness in the long term and right now.

Chapter 11: Homework

This is the last but most important chapter of all. On the other hand, you cannot work on this chapter if you don't have an understanding of the above information. Here, there is some homework for you during the week.

This is an essential component in your self-help therapy, since you will be using what you have already learnt in the previous chapters to fill in your thoughts, feelings, and behaviors before developing steps on how to challenge, cope, and arrive at new strategies.

You will be able to acquire and practice new skills before restructuring the negative beliefs and thinking modes. One may lead you to believe that attending therapy sessions is more important than the homework given. What you need to know is that, even when attending sessions, how you will handle the work given to you is dependent on the effectiveness of the sessions.

If we don't use homework to record our thoughts, insights and plans, then we are at risk of allowing the negative behavior and thoughts to override the opportunity of constructing a new positive way of doing things.

Below, we will help you to attend to the following:

- Capturing negative thoughts

- Recording cognitive distortions

- Dealing with anxiety and stress

- Dealing with anger and depression

- Setting your goals

- Practicing mindfulness

Are you ready? Here is an assignment to go through during the week. Depending on your problem above, fill in on what you need to address.

Capturing Negative Thoughts (NATs)

In a bid to reconstruct your thinking pattern, here is a worksheet for you to fill in when you are ready to capture the negative thoughts. Once you have practiced how to capture negative thoughts in chapter 4, use the information to fill in below.

Situation	NATs	Emotions	Challenging the thought	The balanced thought	Revisit your emotions
Remember the troubling situation	*What negative thought came into your mind as the first reaction?*	*What did you feel? Describe it with one word and rate it with a scale of 0-100%*	*What is the counter thought that is based on factual evidence and challenges the NATs?*	*What was the balancing thought after challenging the NATs?*	*How are your previous emotions now?* *Rate them 0-100%*
Situation 1:					

Situation 2:				

Working on Cognitive Distortions

In chapter 4, we talked about trapping your thoughts. Here is a table to fill in for that. Tick the cognitive distortions that you have been going through and then record how they have been affecting your life against the ticked ones.

If you still do not remember what the words in the cognitive distortion column mean to you, revisit the trapping thoughts section in chapter 4 for more information before filling in the table.

Cognitive distortion	Tick against the one affecting you	Write how the ticked one has affected your life
All or nothing thinking		

Labelling		
Focusing on negativity or filtering your thoughts		
Use of 'should' and 'must' in your to-do statements		
Blame game		
Foretelling		
Overgeneralization		
Mind reading		
Emotional reasoning		
Catastrophizing		
Personalizing		
Jumping to conclusions		

Challenging the Cognitive Distortions

Here, after recording the distortions above, the next table is to help you challenge them. There is an example below each cell to help you in filling it out.

Situation	What did you think?	Cognitive distortion	Emotion	Supporting your emotions	Challenging your thoughts
I did not finish my assignment.	The assignment was too hard. I never found time to do it.	Focusing on the negative.	Stressed, frustrated	I'm a useless person who cannot plan anything or stick to their plan. I simply cannot remember such during the weekend with a party at hand.	I never found time to study. I went to my friend's birthday on the weekend that I was supposed to do it. I need to find time to recover. otherwise it will be too bad.

Dealing with Anxiety and Stress

Here is a table that will help you record your source of stress or anxiety and the alternative thought to challenge the source of the bad thought. It is important that you use logic in reasoning to come up with what happened in the event and what you know to counter the situation.

Stressing/anxious situation or thought	Challenging the thought
Record the anxious thought	Has the anxious thought come into reality at any time in your life?
What made the thought come up in the first place?	If it did happen, what would be the outcome?
How often do I feel this way?	Is there a situation that is most likely going to disprove what you are thinking?

What situation validates the anxiety or stress?	If it happens, what will go on? Is it the worst-case scenario you could be expecting?
Any worst-case scenario about your current feeling?	What do you need to remember about the event that will help you to cool down?

Dealing with Anger and Depression

Do you remember the negative thinking table? Use it to counter depression and angry negative thoughts below.

What are you depressed about? Remember, what is making you angry or depressed?	NATs What negative thought came into your mind?	Emotions What did you feel? Describe it with one word and rate it with a scale of 0-100%	Challenging the thought What is the counter thought that is based on factual evidence and challenges the NATs?	The balanced thought What was the balancing thought after challenging the depression thought?	Revisit your emotions How are your previous emotions now? Rate them 0-100%
Situation 1:					

Situation 2:					

Lastly, here is a table for you to record what you are grateful about every day.

Days	What you are grateful for
Monday	
Tuesday	
Wednesday	

Thursday	
Friday	
Saturday	
Sunday	

Exercise on Goals Setting

Below, record what puts you in a low mood.

What makes me feel low:

Goals after self-help

Remember the SMART model as you answer the following:

- What do you want to gain?

- What do you need to achieve?

- What will be different after attaining your goals?

My goals:

Record the Obstacles
Here, record what you think could prevent you from achieving the set objectives.

What can prevent me from attaining my goals?

Make sure that you overcome the obstacles.

What will I do to make sure that I achieve my objectives?

Practicing Mindfulness

When dealing with your difficulty, it is a good idea to have something that can help you relieve and re-position yourself. Since we tend to get carried away by our thoughts and things to do, having some mindful techniques ready whenever you feel stressed will make sure that you are always a stride ahead of your troubling thoughts, feelings, and behavior.

Here are some mindful meditation tasks that you can utilize next time you feel like it's too much.

Meditation while Walking

- Take a route for a walk. While walking, notice what is around you – the buildings, plants, people, and the accompanying smell. As for the smell, don't go to a route where the smell does not motivate you.

- As you walk, resist the negative thoughts that are bound to take your sensibility away, since you need your senses at the point of walking. Use this time to focus on what is currently happening. Since you are walking, there is nothing to do to settle anything, so you are helping yourself by staying away for a while.

Body Scanning

It is a technique that helps you to come to your senses whenever you feel overwhelmed by thoughts or feelings from a particular situation. Here is how you go about it:

1. Find a quiet place to sit and close your eyes.

2. Start contemplating your body, note your posture position. Where are your hands and feet?

3. Start moving your fingers and toes in a flaring motion. Feel how they all flow and note the stretch they are making on your hands and feet.

4. Now, it's time to roll your head, clockwise three times. As you do it, make sure you are feeling the weight of your head. Were you doing it clockwise? Now do the same in an anticlockwise direction.

5. Next, imagine an electrical impulse travelling in your body. Begin from your toes all the way up to your knees, the hips, your spine, shoulders, before getting to your head. Once it gets on your head, imagine it trickling down in the same manner to your toes where it all began. Repeat one or two more times.

6. Repeat steps 4, 3 and 2 in that order.

7. Once you are done, open your eyes. What's your feeling now?

Object Meditation

Are you a logical or concrete person? It is essential that you utilize what will juice up the senses as you meditate. Use the following in a bid to reposition yourself:

- *Auditory aid:* Some soothing music, tracks with some natural sounds, or white noise.

- *Visual aid:* A moving light that is also changing. It could also include a soothing painting, or just staring at a blank wall.

- *Tangible aid:* A fidget spinner, rubber bands, or yarn.

- *Scented aid:* Cooking, scented candles, fragrances, etc.

At the end of your homework, always remember to work on what you have resolved to do to solve what is troubling your mind. Remember, that is where it all starts.

Conclusion

We all want and need to live a happier life which does not come easy. Before we end the CBT self-help therapy, the question is, how do you condition yourself to live through a complex life with drama all around it?

A sober frame of mind to tackle your feelings and behavior.

At the end of this therapy, you will note many things about yourself, things that you never thought would cross your mind. Remember that you will be judging yourself so that you can scrutinize your problem from all angles and adjust it through changing your thoughts, which in turn changes your feelings and how you behave.

As you learn how to cope with your difficulties, you will be revisiting this book less often since the methods will have stuck from the practice that you have gone through. It is important to understand the importance of practice. The moment you do it for the first two months, you will have captured a wide scope of the problem, plus other related issues that come along. So, whenever negative thoughts pop up, you will be able to counter them using the CBT techniques, and any other useful tools that we have mentioned when maintaining your psychological well-being.

Once you have resolved your problems, it is crucial that you keep the techniques with you until you have fully mastered the art of coping with your issues the right way instead of using negative thoughts. If you are now recovering and moving forward to stay happier, use an exit process that does not make you stop abruptly.

After walking yourself through the steps and techniques, write down a summary of what you have learnt about yourself and your thoughts. It could be on the back of a card that you can put in your wallet. For example, if you learnt how to capture and counter your thoughts, then you have understood that thoughts are not facts and we can choose how to think and react to situations. That is a lesson that you can jot down.

After that you can associate your lesson with the techniques that you came up with to cope with your difficulty. For example, in countering a negative though brought about by stress, you can choose to resolve the stress by walking or listening to soothing music and sounds. That means you have an action plan that you develop to cope with the problem in future when it occurs.

Concerns to Address at the End of Reading

1. Being Able to Cope on Your Own

You are your own boss in this self-help therapy. That means you should be able to cope with the issues affecting your life and overall functionality by practicing the homework assigned. That way, you will allow yourself to always come up with self-talk that enables you to clearly outline the problem and devise the method to make you better and approach the situation with a mind based on factual evidence and a working action plan. Since the lessons are sticking in your head, you should be looking to solve the problems without any help at all, apart from what you have learnt from this therapy.

2. Sorting Out all Your Problems

CBT will not solve all your mental and behavioral problems. On the other hand, it will solve what is listed in the introduction section, and you have the ability to use the skills in the future to work on other issues. Therefore, you should see yourself as a human being who is equipped with life skills to tackle problems when they come.

3. Curing Yourself

Using CBT is not intended to cure the occurrence of negative thoughts or your problem forever. According to Beck, the founder of Cognitive Behavioral Therapy, you need to use the cognitive skills to manage the situation more effectively. When you are managing yourself, the skills become more effective in tackling problematic issues and learning from the tackle for future cases.

4. Addressing the Real Problem

At times, we find ourselves not talking about what is really affecting us. This book is meant for such situations. If you know you are addressing a problem that you are not feeling free to communicate to your friends or therapist, it is possible to view it and solve it on your own with the steps provided. At the end of the day, it is better when we face the real situation instead of beating around the bush and using the skills to solve something unrelated to you.

5. *Looking Forward to a Happier Life*

When therapy is over, and you are feeling alright, at times, you can be faced with the worry that you won't be able to handle yourself outside therapy. You can refer this to as 'falling out' which happens after therapy sessions. Always remind yourself that what you are thinking is not true and you can revisit how to capture negative thoughts and challenge them.

Do you see how CBT techniques can even help you solve how you will be tackling your problems? You also need to note that it is a common problem that many of us face, and working on it is better than submitting to the fear of relapse.

Maintain Your Gains at all Times

Before we conclude, it is essential to address the reason why you need to maintain your achievements. Achieving the gains is easy but we cannot say the same about maintaining them. It is common to think that once you have acquired what you are looking for, the benefits will stick in you magically and forever. From experience, thinking that way will make you fall back on what you solved sooner than you thought.

Therefore, the question you should ask yourself is this: how do you intend to keep the progress that you have developed so far? How many sessions do you need or how many times do you need to revisit the techniques offered in order to guarantee the longevity of what you have learnt?

Have a message that helps you stick to your values, such as 'Use it to live happier and less worried.' Such messages will help you every time you need to troubleshoot future events.

Conclusion

Congratulations on finishing Cognitive Behavioural Therapy, by now you should have a strong understanding towards how you can turn your negative thoughts into positive ones. Enjoy being more confident in yourself, handling future situations the right way and ultimately living a much happier life.

I wish you luck on your journey to health and happiness!

If you found this book helpful please leave a positive review on Amazon as it is greatly appreciated and keeps me being able to deliver high quality books.

www.ingramcontent.com/pod-product-compliance
Lightning Source LLC
Chambersburg PA
CBHW072137020426
42334CB00018B/1841